HEADLINE SERIES

CHINA AT THE CROSSROADS
Reform After Tiananmen

by Steven M. Goldstein

This double issue of the HEADLINE SERIES *has been underwritten by a generous gift from The Henry Luce Foundation, Inc. in the interest of fostering a better understanding of China today.*

1998

The Author

STEVEN M. GOLDSTEIN is professor of government at Smith College, where he has been on
the faculty since 1968. He has also taught at
the Fletcher School of Law and Diplomacy
and at Columbia University, where he earned
his Ph.D. in political science in 1972. A spe-
cialist in Chinese politics and foreign policy,
he commented on developments from
Tiananmen Square in 1989 for CBS News and
CNN. He has written widely on issues ranging
from Sino-Soviet relations to the development of the Communist
movement in China and most recently has edited *The Chinese:
Adapting the Past, Facing the Future* (University of Michigan, Center
for Chinese Studies, 1991) and *Minidragons: Fragile Economic
Miracles in the Pacific* (Westview Press, 1991).

The Foreign Policy Association

The Foreign Policy Association is a private, nonprofit, nonpartisan
educational organization. Its purpose is to stimulate wider interest
and more effective participation in, and greater understanding of,
world affairs among American citizens. Among its activities is the
continuous publication, dating from 1935, of the HEADLINE SERIES.
The author is responsible for factual accuracy and for the views expressed. FPA itself takes no position on issues of U.S. foreign policy.

HEADLINE SERIES (ISSN 0017-8780) is published four times a year, Winter, Spring,
Summer and Fall, by the Foreign Policy Association, Inc., 729 Seventh Ave., New
York, N.Y. 10019. Chairman, Michael H. Coles; President, R.T. Curran; Editor in
Chief, Nancy L. Hoepli; Senior Editors, Ann R. Monjo and K.M. Rohan. Subscription
rates, $15.00 for 4 issues; $25.00 for 8 issues; $30.00 for 12 issues. Single copy price:
$4.00. Price for this double issue: $7.50. Discount 25% on 10 to 99 copies; 30% on
100 to 499; 35% on 500 to 999; 40% on 1,000 or more. Payment must accompany all
orders. Postage and handling: $2.50 for first copy; $.50 each additional copy. Sec-
ond-class postage paid at New York, N.Y. POSTMASTER: Send address changes to
HEADLINE SERIES, Foreign Policy Association, 729 Seventh Ave., New York, N.Y.
10019. Copyright 1992 by Foreign Policy Association, Inc. Design by K.M. Rohan.
Printed at Science Press, Ephrata, Pennsylvania. Double issue: Winter/Spring 1992.
Published October 1992.

Library of Congress Catalog Card No. 92-072962
ISBN 0-87124-148-X

HEADLINE SERIES

No. 298   FOREIGN POLICY ASSOCIATION   Winter/Spring 1992

_951.059_

_G635_

China at the Crossroads
Reform After Tiananmen

by Steven M. Goldstein

Cover Design: Ed Bohon
Photo: AP/Wide World Photos

Double issue: $7.50

$11.25

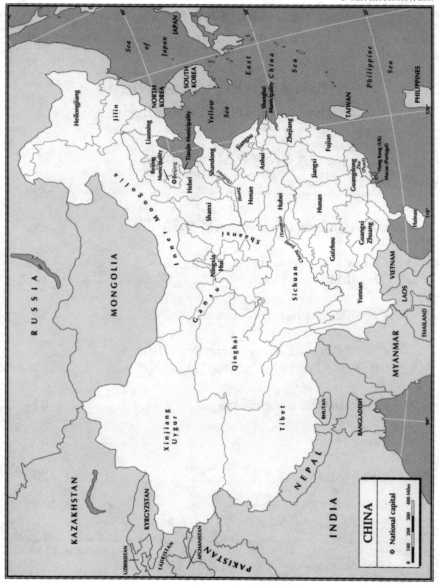

© Current History, Inc.

FOREWORD

Tiananmen Square, 1989

On April 15, 1989, Hu Yaobang died. Hu had been one of Deng Xiaoping's handpicked successors and general secretary of the Chinese Communist party (CCP) until he was forced to resign in 1987. His purge had been the work of party elders (including Deng) who were concerned over student unrest and ideological erosion. Hu had remained on the party's five-member Politburo Standing Committee, however, and had become, in the eyes of many Chinese intellectuals, a symbol of liberalizing tendencies. The fact that he was rumored to have suffered a heart attack while arguing the cause of reform at a party meeting virtually assured his position as a martyr. His death provided a clear justification for students and intellectuals to demonstrate in Tiananmen Square, spiritual center of the nation's capital city, Beijing, just as their predecessors had done when Premier Zhou Enlai died in 1976.

More accurately, one should say it provided yet another justification. Concern over the recent conservative trends in

China's reform movement had motivated some dissidents earlier to make plans for unauthorized demonstrations on May 4, 1989. This was the 70th anniversary of an event of very special significance for Chinese. On that day in 1919, students and intellectuals in Beijing had demonstrated against the accession of the Chinese government to the terms of the Treaty of Versailles that ceded German holdings in China to Japan. It was an outburst of an elite nationalism that had been simmering in China since the turn of the century. Over time, these demonstrations took on a significance that far exceeded their actual scope and size. The May 4th Movement was presented to Chinese youth as the precursor to the Communist revolution as well as the symbol of the willingness of intellectuals to make sacrifices for the good of the nation.

As mourning for Hu began, the first contingent of students arrived at Tiananmen Square. Over the next month and a half, demonstrations spread throughout China to cities such as Shanghai, Xian, Changsha and Chengdu. In Beijing, the numbers in Tiananmen Square grew from less than a thousand to more than a million. Although students and intellectuals were at the core of the demonstrations, they were not the only group protesting. Representatives of China's new entrepreneurs, government bureaucrats, workers and farmers all took to the square as well. Finally, many ordinary citizens of Beijing also came, motivated by everything from simple curiosity to admiration for the students.

Student demands that began as relatively modest in scope soon encompassed calls for China's leaders to resign. Protest tactics also escalated. From the petitions of the early protests, students soon turned to hunger strikes and, finally, to the erection of a 33-foot-tall plaster of Paris and styrofoam "Goddess of Democracy" under the gaze of Mao Zedong's portrait. The affront was not only to Mao, however. It was also to China's current leaders. It was as if demonstrators had occupied the area around the U.S. Capitol in Washington, making it inaccessible to members of Congress or visit-

Tiananmen Square, May 1989: Chinese art students assemble their version of the Statue of Liberty, which they christened the Goddess of Democracy.

© Sheila Phalon

ing dignitaries. And, to make matters worse, foreign television networks in Beijing for the May visit of Soviet President Mikhail S. Gorbachev were able to broadcast the demonstrations (and the Soviet leader's inability to appear in the heart of Beijing) live to enthralled millions around the world.

Curiously, for nearly two months the Chinese leadership did nothing, despite the fact that on April 26 the demonstrations had been condemned as a "planned conspiracy." Such hesitancy can be attributed to concern over the effect of any coercive actions on the international community and to the chilling impact repression might have on China's intellectuals. However, the real deterrent to any action seems to have come from divisions within the upper echelons. From about May 3rd until he was purged later in the month, party leader Zhao Ziyang seems to have argued for a somewhat more conciliatory posture, and this may have delayed action by China's leaders. There is also some indication that as Zhao's position became more difficult, those around him may have encouraged the student demonstrators.

However, there was never any real readiness on the part of China's senior leader Deng Xiaoping to make concessions. In 1986, during the student demonstrations that led to Hu

Yaobang's being forced to step down in 1987, he had made it very clear that the key issue in China's reform was stability:

> Bourgeois liberalization would plunge the country into turmoil once more....The struggle against bourgeois liberalization is also indispensable. We should not be afraid that it will damage our reputation abroad....We must show foreigners that China's political situation is stable. If our country were plunged into disorder and our nation reduced to a heap of loose sand, how could we ever prosper? The reason the imperialists were able to bully us in the past was precisely that we were a heap of loose sand....

Thus, Deng's overarching concern with the importance of stability to China's reform effort should have left little doubt that there would be no compromise with student demands. Moreover, the humiliating fact that the nation's leaders lacked access to their major public buildings during the Sino-Soviet summit, as well as the undoubted sense of Cultural Revolution *déjà vu* that Deng and his colleagues must have felt as masses of people swarmed through the middle of the city, could only have strengthened their resolve to restore order. On May 20 martial law was declared and Zhao Ziyang was effectively purged. On the evening of June 3, the military was directed to restore order in Beijing. Amnesty International has reported that in the crackdown that followed there were at least 1,000 deaths in the capital, while the number of those arrested and detained throughout the country was "much higher" than the figure the government claimed of 4,000.

The demonstrations in Tiananmen Square were a global media event. Television networks broadcast the drama of hunger strikes and massive citizen demonstrations to the living rooms of the United States. After a decade of economic reform in which the face of Maoist communism had undergone a dramatic transformation, it seemed only natural that expectations for further change would be running high and that these heightened hopes would quickly turn to anger when Chinese tanks moved in to clear the demonstrators and police rounded up the leaders of the dissident movement.

Tiananmen thus became one more place name, like the Bastille, to be associated with a turning point in history. The event decisively changed the view of China held by ordinary American citizens as well as many leading politicians. Indeed, very soon thereafter, an "instant wisdom" developed

AFP PHOTO

Deng Xiaoping (center) and his daughter Deng Nan (rear) visited special economic zones in January 1992 to focus attention on his reforms.

regarding the impact that the actions of that night would have on the future of what had earlier been hailed as the pioneer among Communist reform movements.

In regard to the future of China's foreign policy, the images of the foreign business community fleeing Beijing in the days immediately before and after the confrontation at Tiananmen raised serious questions about China's ability to maintain its hard-won reputation as a responsible member of the international economic community. Given the recent uncertainties, would banks continue to extend credits? Would foreign corporations still invest? And what of China's diplomatic credibility or influence? The actions of China's

9

leaders were loudly condemned—particularly in the West. In the eyes of many commentators, China stood a strong chance of being pushed to the margins of world diplomacy and transformed into a global pariah. Indeed, many observers argued that China's leadership might welcome such marginalization. Could a leadership that callously crushed the student movement really care about world opinion? Statements which attributed domestic "disorder" to foreign intrigues were taken by some as portending a return to the inward-looking or self-isolating China of the past.

Domestically, many commentators saw the emergence of a new, antireform, "hard-line Communist" coalition. The evidence for such an assertion was not hard to find. In their justifications for the suppression of the Tiananmen demonstrators, the nation's leaders struck chords that had not been heard in China since before Mao's death. They spoke of a "tiny handful" of people within the Comminist party who "colluded with foreign forces" to subvert communism by inciting "counterrevolutionary rebellion" and promoting "bourgeois liberalization." Even more ominously, by implicating Zhao Ziyang along with a broad range of reform figures and organizations in the anti-Communist turmoil, the post-Tiananmen leadership seemed to be setting the stage for the most extensive and deepest purge since reform began in 1978.

Finally, there was widespread speculation regarding the impact that the Tiananmen crackdown might have on popular support for the regime. Some observers wondered whether the Communist leaders were not facing a loss of popular acceptance and thus the mandate to rule. Indeed, some saw in the proliferation of organized opposition groups signs of the beginnings of a clash between an emerging civil society and an authoritarian state.

For many commentators, what happened at Tiananmen Square contained the seeds of a fundamental shift in the direction of China's politics as well as its relations with the rest of the world. As had occurred before in the history of China, it seemed as if a bold attempt at reform and integration with the world community would be followed by sharp reaction at home and politico-economic isolation abroad. Ironically, just as Eastern Europe and the Soviet Union were starting down a road that would lead to the dismantling of the Communist-socialist political economy, China, after the summer of 1989, appeared to be marching, with determination, in precisely the opposite direction.

Even three years after the event, the images of Tiananmen, and the instant wisdom that developed around them, continue to deeply influence American public opinion and policymakers alike. Relations with China have lost much of the positive momentum that had been building since President Richard M. Nixon's dramatic 1972 visit. Even worse, each side has seemingly fallen back into stereotypes of an earlier era. To some Chinese, U.S. policy has resumed the cold-war cast of Secretaries of State Dean Acheson and John Foster Dulles. Within the United States, the perspective on China has suddenly changed from one of benign support that had been symbolized by Deng Xiaoping's place on the cover of *Time* magazine to one more akin to the anti-Communist stance of the 1950s. Having erroneously crammed the reality of Chinese reform into the simplistic mold of evolving capitalism, are many Americans swinging to the equally simplistic view of orthodox, "hard-line" communism?

In order to formulate an effective policy toward China, Americans must seek a clear understanding of its foreign and domestic policies. It is essential to study the background and causes of the events of June 1989 and to examine the complex evolution of Chinese domestic and foreign policy in the years that followed. It would be unfortunate, indeed, if Sino-American relations were held hostage to an incomplete, or misleading, understanding of China's reform that was born in the emotional aftermath of the demonstrations at Tiananmen.

China's Reform Movement:
The Road to Tiananmen

Mao Zedong, who led China from 1949 until he died in September 1976, left behind a regime that was an amalgam of China's Soviet-style political and economic system of the 1950s and his reforms of the next two decades. The Soviet system was based on the twin pillars of Communist party rule and economic planning. The nineteenth century German political philosopher Karl Marx had asserted that the state represented the ruling class. Vladimir I. Lenin, founder and leader of the Soviet state, maintained that the Communist party represented the best interests of the working class, which was otherwise unable fully to comprehend those interests. Combining these dicta, Soviet communism assumed rule by a self-selected Communist party, unencumbered by checks from a government apparatus, multiparty competition or outside social forces.

In the economic realm, yielding to spontaneous market forces was anathema. Under Soviet dictator Joseph V. Stalin (1929–53), in the Soviet planned economy the overall direction and substance of development were determined by the Communist party leadership and then handed over to a vast bureaucracy to be further assigned to ministries and finally to factories. All goods, from raw materials to agricultural produce to consumer items, were moved through the system by administrative command and not market demand. The absence of a market system spawned a huge economic bureaucracy. It meant that prices bore no relation to scarcity, and managers tended to be more concerned with achieving quotas than with meeting customer demand or turning a profit. Finally, of course, the need to supervise closely production and marshal all resources toward politically determined goals meant there was no room for private enterprise.

During the decade of the 1950s Mao introduced this system to China while he embarked upon an effort to reform it that would preoccupy him for the rest of his life. Some segments of the Soviet system were accepted and even intensified. For example, the emphasis on centralized planning and public ownership fit well with Mao's distaste for the selfish ethos of capitalism. He would hear nothing of private enterprise, markets or profits. However, Mao found other aspects of the Soviet Communist system distasteful. He became convinced that the emphasis on centrally planned economic production slighted the importance of inculcating socialist values in the population and bred a class of privileged bureaucrats and intellectuals. In order to avoid this outcome, Mao sought to weaken bureaucratic hierarchies, to impose ideological strictures and egalitarian life-styles on the people, and to attack the nation's intellectuals.

The political and economic system that Mao left his heirs was rife with the contradictions that had resulted from nearly two decades of experimentation and reform. It was a system which sought economic growth for the sake of national strength but which also reflected the concern that too great an emphasis on growth or on the use of material rewards to motivate workers would result in the restoration of capitalism. For Mao, class struggle with the bourgeoisie remained the primary task, even after the revolution that brought the Communists to power in 1949. To carry on the struggle, he emphasized the need for an intrusive government that would regulate the nation's economy as well as the living habits and thinking of its people. However, Mao's attacks on the Communist party-state bureaucracy also weakened its internal discipline and effectiveness as a national institution, giving an arbitrary quality to its intrusive role. Finally, even as he attacked China's intellectuals as inherently anti-Communist, he looked to his country to develop its own technology and avoid reliance on foreign nations.

As in the Soviet Union at the time of Stalin's death in 1953, there was a widespread mandate for change both within the bureaucracy and among the populace when Mao died. Bureaucrats sought stability while much of the general public sought not only a respite from the incessant ideological campaigns but also an end to more than a decade of stagnating living standards. However, what set China apart from the Soviet Union was the people who made up the nation's elite. When Stalin died, he was survived by none of the old Bolshevik revolutionaries who had opposed his policies of the previous three decades. His successors, men like Georgi M. Malenkov, Lavrenti P. Beria and Nikita S. Khrushchev, were not only Stalin's creations, they were the beneficiaries of his policies. They had to move gingerly in condemning the system that had not only produced them but had rewarded them generously.

After Mao's death, the situation in China was very different. Many who survived him were individuals of considerable party seniority who had been his opponents as well as the victims of his policies. For example, the economist Chen Yun had been seeking innovative solutions for China's Communist system since the 1960s—running afoul of Mao's Great Leap Forward, the 1958–60 economic program to raise rapidly industrial and agricultural production, and his Cultural Revolution (the movement which set China on a course of political and social disorder for a decade until Mao's death)

14

in the process. Deng Xiaoping was a major target of the Cultural Revolution and enjoyed the dubious distinction of having been rehabilitated in 1973 only to be purged again in 1976 when he sought to redirect some of the more radical Maoist economic policies.

The Dilemmas of Reform

Given their experiences with Mao and his policies, it was understandable that Deng and his colleagues moved swiftly to deal with the late leader's legacy. The Cultural Revolution was quickly adjudged to have been an error resulting, in large part, from Mao's increasing radicalism in the last two decades of his life. Deng and his colleagues declared that major class struggles were over and that the nation had to focus its attention and energies on the business of economic development. To stimulate economic growth, workers' wages were increased for the first time in more than a decade; collective-farm purchase prices were raised; intellectuals were encouraged to contribute their talents as members of the working class (not as potential class enemies, as had been the case under Mao); and earlier strictures against cultivating ties with the global economy were repudiated.

With Chen Yun's return, the Chinese press was filled with long suppressed proposals for the reform of all aspects of the Communist economy. Like their counterparts in Eastern Europe, Chinese economists pointed to the pathologies that stood in the way of greater economic efficiency: a planning apparatus and process that could no longer integrate the demands of a complex economy; prices that did not reflect scarcity values; sectoral imbalances; enterprises that had little incentive or ability to innovate to meet customer needs, etc. Their solutions were also typical of reform proposals throughout the Communist world: allowing some room for a market economy that, in turn, meant real prices, greater enterprise initiative, looser state control, some privatization, economic criteria for performance, reallocation of resources from previously favored sectors, etc.

Yet this awareness of the need for reform was offset by a sensitivity to the difficulties of implementing it as well as by a lack of consensus within the leadership regarding possible limits. The obstacles were as formidable in China as they have been in other Communist countries. The system's dependence on centrally controlled economic management meant that there were hundreds of thousands of bureaucrats at all levels who had a vested interest in the continuation of the old system. For factory managers who had long been accustomed to simply filling government orders from state-provided raw materials—with little regard for marketability or profitability—the uncertainties of adapting to market signals were daunting. Workers who complained about low standards of living benefited from the security provided by a Communist industrial system that provided a wide range of factory subsidized services—housing, child care, education, meals, social security—as well as the assurance of lifetime employment (an "iron rice bowl") in an enterprise that never had to face the prospect of bankruptcy. Outside the factories, these workers, along with the entire urban population, benefited from the state-fixed prices on food and services that were far below their market value. In exchange for its inefficiencies in overall performance, the Soviet-style system provided millions of Chinese with economic security.

No wonder then that the reformer's role has been such a difficult one in Communist systems. For even with widespread agreement on the need to implement reform to increase overall economic productivity and raise living standards in the long run, few groups in society are willing to learn new patterns of behavior, to suffer the employment uncertainties of trial by market or to endure the inevitable inflation that comes from the introduction of higher, "real" prices that reflect scarcity value. A thoroughgoing reform effort inevitably runs the risks of widespread political opposition and social instability. Given this reality, it is not surprising that Gorbachev and his East European colleagues frequently chose to muddle through or that the post-Commu-

Workman scrubs a new portrait of Mao Zedong on the Gate of Heavenly Peace. The portrait replaces one that was defaced during May 1989 demonstrations.

Reuters/Bettmann

nist regimes, now making the transition to market economies, confront considerable popular nostalgia for the security of the "bad old days."

The Chinese reformers of the 1980s were aware of these pitfalls. And their attitude toward the reform of the Soviet-style fundamentals of the economy was clearly different from their attitude toward change of its Maoist aspects. The decade would show that their agreement on what had to be done was fragile, largely because of the vague goals they had for reform. Deng and his colleagues had some sense of what the problems were, but they had no overarching plan for reform. Rather they settled for such adages as Chen Yun's comparison of the economy under state regulation to a bird in a cage—if the cage were too small the bird would die; if the cage were too large, the bird would fly away.

Indeed, Deng's depiction of reform as crossing a stream feeling for the rocks was a good approximation of the process by which the program evolved. Not only did it proceed in an often *ad hoc* manner, but the desire to cushion the shocks of change meant that reformers often went one step at a time, leaving one foot securely planted in the familiar policies of the Communist system as they moved the other forward to the uncertainties of the market economy. This approach would often yield dramatic results, but the lack of leadership consensus, as well as the often improvisational and partial nature of the reforms, would do grievous damage to the reform process in China.

Content of the Pre-Tiananmen Reforms

The Economy. The most dramatic and decisive reforms during the decade of the 1980s took place in agriculture. Under Mao, China had copied (and even intensified) the Stalinist approach to agriculture. Peasants—more than 80 percent of the population—were organized into collective units that determined what would be produced and how. Except for occasionally sanctioned private plots and rural markets, all work was centered in these units and all produce was sold by the collective to the state at set prices. The government's desire to maximize funds available for industry meant that it kept purchase prices low and limited overall investment in agriculture. Rural work was regimented, labor intensive and poorly paid. Scholars have estimated that by the late 1970s, per capita income in the cities was between three to six times that in the countryside.

Between 1978 and 1989 agricultural reform went through three stages. In the first two years, the emphasis was mostly on allocating greater financial resources to agriculture while keeping its collectivist organizational structure intact. Investment in infrastructure and the price paid by the state to the collectivized peasantry for their production were increased. By the early 1980s, agricultural reform had moved into a second stage that entailed the virtual decollectivization of agriculture. Under the "household-responsibility system," collective structures were abolished and land was allocated to families who, in return, were expected to provide a fixed-sales quota of grain to the state and a share of the community's taxes. Anything above that quota could be sold on the emerging markets or to the state at premium prices. Finally, peasants were allowed either privately or collectively to establish manufacturing or service enterprises.

The response to these changes, which restored the family as the basic production unit, was dramatic. By 1984 grain output had reached an all-time high of 407 million metric tons. However, this was not necessarily good news. Since the state was committed to purchase all grain produced and to sell it to the cities at a lower subsidized price, agricultural successes were, ironically, depleting an already strained treasury. The third stage of reform—the "contract-responsibility system" of 1985—was a response to this situation: henceforth the state would no longer stand ready to purchase all production. It would contract with peasant families for a fixed portion of their production at a state-determined price. The rest could be sold for the families' own accounts on rural or urban markets. Eventually, it was anticipated, more and more of the agricultural produce would be distributed through the emerging market system. In short, by the late 1980s the two pillars of the collective system had been abolished. China's peasants now worked small family farms, were expected to buy much of their inputs (seeds, fertilizer, etc.) on the open market, and could sell significant portions of their harvest at higher open-market prices. However, the role of the state persisted: it provided limited inputs and saw to it that sales contracts with the government were met.

Reforms in the foreign economic sector were equally dramatic. Soviet foreign trade theory, as well as Mao's obsession with the dangers of China's penetration by foreign ideas and foreign economic forces, had created a policy characterized by one Chinese commentator as "filling gaps in domestic supply." After Mao's death, his successors moved quickly to reverse this pattern, making involvement in the international economic system an integral part of the nation's

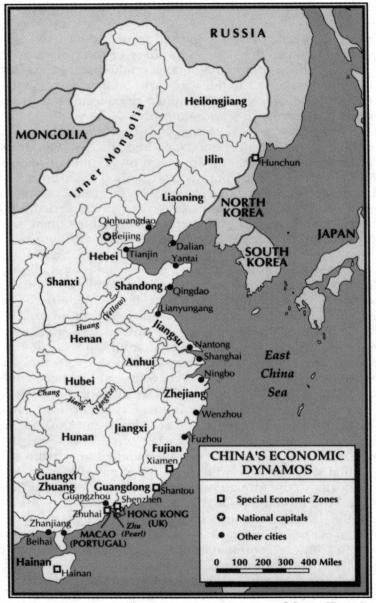

RUSSIA

MONGOLIA

Heilongjiang

Inner Mongolia

Jilin

□ Hunchun

Liaoning

NORTH KOREA

Qinhuangdao

✪ Beijing

Hebei   Tianjin

Dalian
Yantai

SOUTH KOREA

JAPAN

Shanxi

Shandong

Qingdao

Lianyungang

Huang (Yellow)

Jiangsu

Henan

Nantong

Anhui

Shanghai

Hubei

Ningbo

Chang Huang (Yangtze)

Zhejiang

East China Sea

Jiangxi

Wenzhou

Hunan

Fujian

Fuzhou

Xiamen □

Guangxi Zhuang

Guangdong □ Shantou

Guangzhou   Shenzhen

Zhuhai □

HONG KONG (UK)

Zhanjiang

Zhu (Pearl)

MACAO (PORTUGAL)

Beihai

Hainan

Hainan □

CHINA'S ECONOMIC DYNAMOS

□ Special Economic Zones

✪ National capitals

● Other cities

0   100 200 300 400 Miles

development strategy. In the process of purchasing needed technology abroad, China's leaders almost immediately expanded the nation's foreign trade. Although exports could pay part of the bill, it soon became apparent that China would have to break longstanding strictures on borrowing abroad.

In 1979, Deng and his colleagues broke yet another taboo, opening the nation to direct foreign investment. At first, such investment was limited to four "special economic zones" (SEZs—Shenzhen, Zhuhai, Shantou and Xiamen). In 1984, a second step was taken when 14 Chinese coastal cities and Hainan island were authorized to seek investment from abroad and to provide special tax incentives to foreign entrepreneurs. The third step came in 1988, when the then Communist party general secretary Zhao Ziyang announced a plan to seek foreign investment aggressively along China's coast—the so-called export-led coastal development strategy, or gold-coast campaign. Finally, throughout these years China sought aid for its development from international agencies ranging from the United Nations to the Asian Development Bank to the World Bank.

In their public statements, at least, China's leaders argued that success in agriculture and foreign trade and investment would be the stimulus for reform in a third area, the urban industrial sector. This began in the early 1980s with the granting of greater autonomy to factories and localities. China's counties, cities and provinces were given greater control over economic activity and were allowed to keep a greater share of industrial revenue.

In 1984, a comprehensive plan was unveiled aimed at achieving some combination of centralized planning and a free market for the urban economy. In the years that followed steps were taken to establish a system in which some prices were set by the state, others fluctuated within state-set boundaries and still others were set by market demand. Ministries were to provide only a limited amount of raw materials and assign much smaller production quotas to enterprises that were granted the right to sell over-quota production at much higher market prices. This privilege, it was hoped, would encourage market-economy-like behavior by the firms in seeking sources of raw materials and customers, and would promote more-entrepreneurial behavior among Chinese managers. There was even discussion of alleviating factory overstaffing through lay-offs and allowing inefficient enterprises to go bankrupt.

The program to "enliven" the economy went beyond giving more power to local governments and enterprises, however. Patterns of ownership were expanded. There was talk of opening stock exchanges in China and, for the first time since the early 1950s, positive encouragement was given to private and cooperative enterprise. Yet, once again, as with the rural economy, the state sector remained a strong presence, employing 70 percent of the urban population in large state factories, fixing the prices of many key items and maintaining direct control of most of the country's essential industries.

The Political System. A major thrust of the political reform under Deng was to put to rest the memory and ideology of the Cultural Revolution period. In 1981, the Communist party issued its official judgment on that period, condemning most policies and placing primary blame for them upon Mao himself. As they discarded much of the ideology of the Maoist period, China's leaders sought to find a new basis for the regime by emphasizing the party's accomplishments and its central mission of economic growth. Borrowing from Marxism, Zhao Ziyang in the mid-1980s had characterized China's economic development as being in the "primary stage of socialism"—a stage where the major task facing a Communist state is improved economic performance and living standards, but not class struggle.

The importance placed on economic development was also apparent in the reforms of the political structure that attempted to relax the administration's grip. For those bureaucracies that continued to function, the reformers had three goals: streamlining, the replacement of old and ineffective cadres with younger, better-educated individuals, and the reimposition of discipline. Lean, well-staffed and honest bureaucracies were seen as a necessary prerequisite for China's economic development.

Clarifying the demarcation of responsibilities among bureaucracies was another goal of the 1978–89 political reform movement. In regard to civil-military relations, Deng worked to bring the military under the control of civilian authorities and to lessen defense expenditures while building a modern professional army. There was some talk of getting the Communist party out of the management of daily life, ceding greater authority to legislative bodies or factory management. There were even proposals in 1987 to diminish the staffing powers of the Communist party. In the fall of that year Zhao Ziyang proposed the creation of a civil service system to appoint "those doing professional work." Of course, little real diminution of party power was anticipated. The Communist party would still maintain overall "political leadership" and appoint crucial cadres.

The limits to this vision of political reform are obvious. Deng was seeking to create a more efficient, but nonetheless party-dominated, authoritarian system. While decisionmaking would become more open and regularized, it would remain the privilege of an elite. Deng and his colleagues were not prepared to cede to society the right to set the political agenda or to choose its leaders. Communist democracy had little to do with human rights or popular choice. As Deng himself suggested in 1986, strong Communist party leadership was essential to successful economic reform and the maintenance of China's international position.

This did not mean that an individual's life remained as regulated as it had been under Mao, however. In areas ranging from dress to the arts to hobbies, permissible bounds were expanded. Moreover, the reformers sought to alleviate popular cynicism toward politics by strengthening legal safeguards against bureaucratic abuses and by stimulating participation in multicandidate local elections. In the words of one Western observer, China seemed to be "coming alive."

Despite these widened boundaries, it was clear that some things had not changed since the beginning of the reform movement with respect to the relationship between the individual and the political system. In early 1979, Deng asserted that only those statements and activities that upheld the "four cardinal principles"—maintaining socialism and supporting the people's democratic dictatorship, leadership by the Communist party, and Marxism-Leninism/Mao Zedong thought—would be permitted. To allow the populace to influence the political agenda, he maintained, would only result in the unravelling of communism in China, namely "bourgeois liberalization." In Deng's view, authoritarian Communist party leadership was necessary if China's economic reform was to succeed. While he was prepared to allow a limited marketplace for the exchange of economic goods, there would be little marketplace for the exchange of unsanctioned ideas.

From the overview above, it appears as if Deng and his colleagues were carrying out bolder reforms in the economic sector than in the political realm. However, as Yasheng Huang of the University of Michigan has noted, even the economic reforms were partial in nature. In the industrial and rural sectors, elements of the previous command economy coexisted with elements of the market system. Seeking to maintain the stability of government control during the transition to the free market, the reformers created a system that remained in limbo somewhere between partially planned and market economy—a foot on each stone, to borrow Deng's analogy. And as the events in Tiananmen Square would demonstrate, this was a very dangerous situation indeed.

A Decade of Reform

Accomplishments. In late March of 1989, the National People's Congress of China was preparing to meet. Although recently it had shown signs of growing assertiveness, this body still exercised few of the constitutional powers vested in it as the nation's highest law-making body. However, its meetings provided the opportunity for China's leaders to report on the state of the nation. And, as reform entered the first year of its second decade, there was much to substantiate Premier Li Peng's proud assertion in his opening speech that in the "past 10 years tremendous changes of historic significance had taken place in all aspects of life in China." The reforms were clearly bearing fruit.

As one official publication put it, although it still had a long way to go, China was "bridging the economic gap" between itself and the rest of the world. Gross national product (GNP) had increased during the early 1980s at an annual rate more that twice that of Japan and four times that of the United States. Chinese industry was growing at 11 percent per year. In agriculture, cereal goods were said to have grown at three times the annual world average over the reform decade while meat output reportedly increased at a yearly rate of more than eight times that average.

One could also detect signs that the grip of the state planning system was being relaxed. It has been estimated that by the mid-1980s, the number of industrial goods allocated through the mandatory planning system was 10 percent of what it had been in the 1950s, with most items being distributed through contractual arrangements. The number of goods sold at state-fixed prices was also reduced to the point that it constituted only between 30 percent and 40 percent of total sales. Finally, Chinese, either individually or as part of a collective, were rushing to take advantage of the liberalized regulations regarding ownership by opening everything from small service establishments to construction companies and factories. In 1988, while state enterprises grew at an annual rate of 13 percent, collective enterprises grew at 29 percent and private enterprises at an amazing 46 percent.

Life was also changing for the ordinary Chinese citizen. According to official statistics, the Chinese people were living far better than they had a decade before. In the cities, per capita income had grown at an annual rate of nearly 13 percent between 1978 and 1987, with urban dwellers now able to purchase such coveted consumer items as refrigerators, cassette recorders and television sets. In the countryside, per capita income was growing at a rate of nearly 15 percent a year, with similar improvement in living standards.

Equally welcome were the results of liberalization in the cultural sphere. Western clothing was commonplace, as were American television serials, Hong Kong music and traditional Chinese opera. Although the CCP remained suspicious of intellectuals, the literary and performing arts were flourishing. And, perhaps most importantly, by 1988, 150,000 visas reportedly had been issued for study abroad.

Finally, the decade had also witnessed impressive international economic achievements for China. According to figures released by the Chinese government, two-way foreign trade had gone from $29 billion in 1979 to $79 billion in 1988. During the previous decade, it was reported, China had negotiated loan agreements valued at $47 billion and had used almost 75 percent of that available credit. Nearly 16,000 foreign-funded enterprises, representing a foreign investment of $25 billion, had been approved, with almost a third already in operation. Finally, China was exploiting the support available from international organizations. It was receiving more support from the UN Development Program than any other country in the world and had received more than $8.7 billion in World Bank assistance.

Challenges. In light of all these domestic and international accomplishments, few of the delegates listening to Li Peng that March day could have detected signs of the grave crisis that would soon result in mass demonstrations and an ugly military confrontation under the windows of the very building in which they sat. Yet, with the advantage of hindsight, it is possible to detect the roots of the Tiananmen demonstrations in many of the accomplishments of the decade of reform. Some of the most serious problems were implicitly acknowledged by the premier himself when he announced that the reform task for the next few years would be "to focus on improvement and rectification" of the economy. In plain language, to borrow the characterization of a Central Intelligence Agency (CIA) report that described the state of the Chinese economy during the previous months, Li was saying that reforms would be put "on hold."

The need for a respite had become apparent during the summer and fall of 1988. That year China's industrial production had grown by 21 percent, with the most dramatic increases occurring in those areas of the economy unleashed by the reform policies.

Given China's economic condition, such rapid growth was by no means good news. The existence of a private sector within an overwhelmingly state-dominated economy not only generated social tensions by increasing economic disparities among a population unaccustomed to such differentiation, but it also provided numerous opportunities for corruption. Those with connections—usually officials or their children—could benefit from their special access to permits, contracts, materials or foreign business people in establishing private or cooperative enterprises. Meanwhile, the efficiency and profitability of state enterprises were suffering from the uncertainties of supply and demand created by the new mixed system. Even in state enterprises there were abundant opportunities for corruption. The existence of dual pricing, in which the price of some goods was determined in the marketplace and that of others was set by the state, was an invitation to profitable manipulation by officials who diverted underpriced but scarce state-supplied goods into the expanding marketplace. The profits grew as the nation found itself slipping into a period of spiraling inflation.

These inflationary pressures were, in part, the product of another result of reform policies: ambitious local industrialization. The officials in China's counties, cities and provinces sought to build industries to provide employment, to raise tax revenues and to enhance local prestige. The result was the sprouting of redundant production lines for such items as refrigerators and color televisions that far exceeded the country's needs. In addition, the factories' demand for scarce resources drove up their prices in the new, limited market system, while local financial institutions generated credit to assist in financing their purchase. With rural industry clearly more profitable than agriculture, many farmers took advantage of their newfound freedom to move into other, more lucrative, areas. In 1988 grain production actually fell for the first time since the reform had begun.

Amid these developments, a tentative decision—in retrospect ill-conceived—was made in the spring of 1988 to move ahead with price reform, allowing the growing inflationary pressures to hit the Chinese consumer. By August–September the cumulative effects of the announced price reform on the overheated economy were apparent. Nationally, inflation ran as high as 19 percent a year; the rate in the urban areas reached 30 percent. The resultant panic buying was a severe blow to the authority of a government that prided itself on having brought price stability to a nation that, in the late 1940s, had suffered through one of the worst inflations of the twentieth century.

And that was not all. With prices of industrial raw materials and food rising, always-unprofitable state industries began to lose even more money while consumers faced increasing food prices. The state, although suffering from reduced revenue collections due to local retention of tax money, increased its subsidies to the unprofitable enterprises and the financially strapped consumers. The result was a large budget deficit that was addressed by printing more money—further fueling the inflationary spiral.

In agriculture a quieter crisis was brewing. Investment in such essential areas as irrigation had declined due to the dissolution of collective structures and peasant unwillingness to invest in land they feared might be taken away in some future swing of the policy pendulum. Facing the uncertainties of the evolving state grain market, many rural families devoted their energies to other crops or to local industries.

Ranan R. Lurie, Cartoonews International Syndicate, NYC

State grain-purchase prices were simply too low and production inputs too expensive and unreliable to obtain. Finally, many rural people were angered at the success of some of their neighbors as well as at the former collective cadres who took advantage of their special position to profit from the establishment of local enterprises or from trading in such goods as seeds and fertilizers.

By mid-1988, with the economy seemingly on the verge of getting out of control, many Chinese leaders concluded that reform had gone too far. While some were willing to risk greater social instability as a necessary price for change, others, such as Chen Yun, were concerned over the destabilizing impact of further reform and argued for a slowing down of the process. As the chief advocate for reform, Zhao Ziyang took the brunt of the blame for the crisis. In September 1988, the responsibility for bringing China's economy under control fell to the more conservative premier, Li Peng. In the months that followed, he presided over efforts to slow, as well as to control, economic growth by cutting investment, reasserting central control over investment and raw material distribution, and reestablishing price controls.

When Li stood before the National People's Congress almost six months later, it was clear that these actions had not really solved the problems confronting China. Corruption and inequality persisted. Economic growth had been slowed, but double-digit inflation continued. Standards of living in the urban areas were leveling off or even falling slightly. With education underfunded and government stipends relatively fixed, students, intellectuals and government workers were feeling the economic pinch. Workers, previously guaranteed employment for life, were additionally uneasy over the contracting economy and continued talk of cutting back in economically inefficient enterprises. In the week that the congress ended its session, the official magazine, *Beijing Review,* expressed a concern on many people's minds when it ran an article entitled "Does China Face Stagflation?"

More significantly, certain reform-minded groups in society—particularly the students and critical intellectuals—were becoming increasingly uneasy over the growing prominence of conservative politicians and policies. Adding fuel to an already volatile situation, they demanded in public statements and letters to the leadership that languishing political reform be accelerated in the direction of "political democratization" and the protection of human rights. Despite the widened boundaries for citizen behavior noted earlier, it was clear from the beginning of the reform movement that there would be little tolerance for such demands. Even General Secretary Zhao, who was widely regarded as Hu Yaobang's successor as party liberal, argued that China, like South Korea and Taiwan, needed a "neo-authoritarian" regime to guide its modernization. By raising the issue of political democratization, China's intellectuals were on a collision course with the leadership just as the reform movement reached a critical, and potentially dangerous, juncture.

Tiananmen: The Fruits of Reform

Reformist leaders in Soviet-type systems face a central dilemma: the political and social tensions created by reform often are more threatening to the regime than the dangers of muddling through with an unreformed system. The Chinese attempt at reform during the decade of the 1980s not only proves this axiom, but adds a corollary, suggested by Professor Huang: partial reform can often make things worse. In Tiananmen Square, one might say, broad social tensions generated by a decade of reform spilled into the streets.

For the leaders of the demonstrations, the partial reform bred three kinds of grievances. The first was inflation, in great measure a result of the partial restructuring of the price system, the granting of greater autonomy to localities and the state's commitment to continuing to provide subsidies to cushion the impact of needed price adjustments. The second related to the opportunities for corruption that resulted from an economic system that allowed private entrepreneurial activity while it maintained a strong element of state control. These ranged from the profits that could be made from buying goods at state prices and selling them on the free markets to using family connections for private gain, with particular ire directed at the advantages enjoyed by the sons and daughters of high cadres.

The final way in which partial reform fed the demonstrations was the commonly cited discrepancy between political and economic relaxation. There is some truth to the contention that a decade of reform had fueled the crisis by generating rising expectations for political change that were unacceptable to China's very Leninist leaders. However, it is also true that, despite the widely held view in the West, these were not "pro-democracy" demonstrators. Many of the demonstrations' leaders shared the party chiefs' belief in the importance of elite-guided government in China. They simply felt that the Communist movement had exhausted its organizational and ideological potential. Like the May 4th demonstrators of 1919, they believed that it was time for new leaders to emerge from among China's intellectuals to take up the cause of national salvation.

Because they held to this view, the leaders of the demonstration perhaps failed to use effectively the widespread social unrest generated by the reform movement that had caused millions to take to the streets in Beijing and other cities. China's new entrepreneurs, frustrated by their dealings with a predatory bureaucracy, lent their support. Bureaucrats concerned with their declining prestige and standard of living amid inflation appeared in the square as did workers, also upset over the inflation as well as the possibility of lessened job security in a more-market-oriented economy. Thus, while reform policies generated social tensions, not all demonstrators took to the streets to promote reform. As Martin K. Whyte of the University of Michigan has noted, even as students voiced their support for reform, workers and bureaucrats seemed more concerned that it might continue and so erode their position. What most demonstrators did unite around was a shared unhappiness with the most obvious results of reform—economic inequality, inflation, corruption and nepotism.

Social tensions are the inevitable by-product of reform in Communist states as vital interests are endangered and norms are challenged. Reform in a Communist system inevitably creates advocates and opponents. For those tensions to be contained or even channeled in constructive ways requires a united and firm leadership. Leadership division or inaction, on the other hand, invites escalation. The course of reform had not only eroded China's social stability but it had also eroded the unity of its leaders and their determination to persevere on the path of reform. In the spring of 1989, their inaction only bred greater boldness on the part of the demonstrators. And, as the demonstrations persisted, it became easier for Deng and most of his colleagues to act on what was their lowest common denominator of consensus: continued "turmoil" (*luan*) would lead to foreign interference and the overthrow of communism. On June 3–4, order was brutally restored. However, the lesson of Tiananmen Square—that reform bred instability—was not lost on the Chinese leaders. It was clearly on their minds as they pondered the next step.

Post-Tiananmen Reform

For more than two years after the Tiananmen Square demonstrations, the reform process faltered. Contrary to widespread belief, it did not backtrack. While there was significant progress in certain areas, the earlier momentum seemed to have been lost—a victim of political and social deadlock.

In late 1991 and early 1992 the mood changed dramatically as Deng intervened to break that stalemate. Reform themes were raised with a stridency and boldness that had not been heard since the heady days of 1987–88. Deng was seeking to achieve an ambitious agenda dominated by the two key issues that had eluded him in the past: the launching of a reform movement combining economic structural change with political stability and the creation of an arrangement for succession that would ensure that those who followed him would stay the course of reform. It is clearly Deng's last hurrah in Chinese politics.

Economic Reform: Suspended or Reversed?

For a full nine months before the Tiananmen outburst, it was clear that uncontrolled growth and inflation were pushing the Chinese economy to the brink of crisis and that those who wanted to slow the pace of reform were taking charge of its day-to-day management. In these months, the outlines of a retrenchment program emerged, although there seemed to be political difficulties in carrying out some of the specific policies. The disturbances at Tiananmen Square removed many of these difficulties. The shock of the outcries gave a powerful impetus for a more vigorous curtailment and weakened many—but not all—of the leaders and institutions that might have resisted this process. China moved into an uncertain period during which the stated goal was that of "improving the economic environment and rectifying the economic order."

In effect, China's post-Tiananmen leadership implemented a strict austerity program that rapidly deflated the economy and effectively pushed it into recession. State enterprises, accustomed to free-flowing credit, suddenly found themselves without cash to pay suppliers and employees. Soon the Chinese industrial economy became ensnared in a series of "debt chains" where the inability of one firm to pay its debts undermined its suppliers, causing them to default, in turn, to their suppliers, etc. By 1990 unsold inventories were piling up and firms were laying off workers or suspending operations. Almost one fifth of China's industrial enterprises had closed. In the rural areas, local food processing, small-appliance and textile industries also felt the deflationary crunch. Millions of farmers were forced to return to agricultural work as a result of factory closings. Foreign trade seemed to have been brought under some control with the country's trade deficit erased and its foreign reserves enhanced. Finally, of course, the most important goal of the austerity program was to reduce the double-digit inflation that was threatening popular support for the government. And here the results were remarkable, as the monthly inflation rate dipped below 5 percent at the beginning of 1990. Price stability seemed once more a fact in China.

Ironically, by mid-1990, the gains of the austerity program were threatening the social stability which it was intended to buttress. As Barry Naughton of the University of California at San Diego has noted, the program had created an economic crisis with the potential to trigger precisely the social unrest that China's leaders had sought to avoid. This concern was intensified by the developments in Eastern Europe as popular movements toppled one Communist regime after the other. As real incomes declined, unemployment grew and consumer confidence waned, something had to be done.

The result was an effort to reinflate the economy by providing credit, subsidizing inefficient factories and relaxing some of the strictures on state investment and local industry. By mid-1991, it was reported that China's industry had grown by more than 13 percent—a figure approaching that of the years before the Tiananmen crisis. Moreover, the relaxed restrictions on private and rural industry produced a pattern of growth similar to that of the reform years. By the end of 1991, it was reported that rural industries were employing close to 100 million workers, many of whom had earlier returned to farming.

For commentators in the West, the 1989–91 cycle seemed to repeat the boom/bust cycle that had characterized post-1978 economic growth. A. Doak Barnett, dean of America's China-watchers, noted that the Chinese government had proven once more that it could deflate the economy during periods of overheating and stimulate it during periods of recession. What was by no means clear, however, was whether it could formulate policies that could create the sustained growth to avoid these cycles. Did the post-Tiananmen retrenchment program show any signs of new policy directions?

One direction in which policy did *not* go was back to the Soviet-style planned economy of the 1950s and 1960s. On the contrary, the leadership spoke of its determination to continue with reform once stability had returned. Most significantly, with the exception of the forbidden topic of privatization, vigorous discussion of economic reform continued in the Chinese press.

If, contradictory to widely held beliefs, the reform movement lost little ground after the Tiananmen demonstrations, did it make any progress? Some have argued that bringing the inflation and hypergrowth of the late 1980s under control was an achievement. However, accomplishments went beyond mere stabilization. In at least three areas, as the economist Nicholas R. Lardy of the University of Washington has noted, there was positive reform momentum in the two years following the summer of 1989.

Price Reform, Expanding Entrepreneurial Sector and Foreign Trade. The first was the continuing movement toward price reform and a market economy. There were adjustments in state-fixed prices of coal, transportation and certain items in the urban food basket that state planners had kept artificially low. More radical were the steps taken to foster prices that more accurately reflected market signals through the expansion of a three-tier price system. The latter consisted of traditional state-fixed prices, prices set by supply and demand and prices permitted to fluctuate between upper and lower limits set by the state. According to an October 1991 report in the official Communist party daily, *Renmin Ribao,* the proportion of goods circulating at these three types of prices were, respectively, 30 percent, 53 percent and 17 percent for retail sales; 25 percent, 52 percent and 23 percent for food items; and 44 percent, 19 percent and 37 percent for capital goods.

The price structure described above suggests that the central planners were allocating less than half of the goods produced. The rest were being bought and sold by contract between firms or in the many markets for food and other goods that were springing up throughout China. By late 1991, the market system had further developed to encompass foreign-currency trading, regional wholesale markets

© Sheila Phalon

May 1989: The press, radio and television cover the demonstrations in Tiananmen Square.

for nonferrous metals and agricultural futures, and two small stock exchanges.

A second area of reform progress is what Lardy calls the Chinese economy's "entrepreneurial sector": the collective, private and foreign-financed firms not under the direct management of the planning bureaucracy. What sets these firms apart from those in the state sector is not simply their place in the national bureaucratic hierarchy, but, even more important, their manner of doing business. Unlike state enterprises, they raise their own capital, seek their own suppliers, set their own wage bills and sell their goods on competitive markets. The strength of these firms is, of course, one indication of the extent to which the market system is permitted in the economy. And their rapid growth, as well as the fact that their output represented 45 percent of manufactured goods in 1990, suggests the continuing health of market-oriented businesses in the post-Tiananmen period.

Finally, there is foreign trade. Proposals in the fall of 1989 to centralize and limit foreign economic relations and to assure greater equality in regional growth all seemed to undercut Zhao's gold-coast strategy that emphasized an "open door" policy and granted coastal provinces considerable foreign trade autonomy. By 1990, it was clear that there would be little pullback in regard to foreign economic relations, and the post-Tiananmen leadership, facing resistance from the coastal provinces to any reduction of their special privileges, returned to Zhao's strategy. In the first eight months of 1991, the Chinese government reported that foreign investment had increased by 55 percent over the previous year (exceeding a record set in 1985), foreign borrowings were up 32 percent, foreign-exchange holdings had doubled and exports had increased by 18 percent.

Perhaps more significantly, the two coastal provinces of Fujian (opposite Taiwan) and Guangdong (adjacent to Hong Kong) had garnered more than half the foreign investment in China. The impact on their economies was dramatic. In 1990–91, Guangdong enjoyed the most rapid industrial growth in China (and, possibly, in all Asia), along with double-digit growth in per capita income and foreign trade. Perhaps equally significant was the report that, within this most rapidly growing economy, the production of state-sector industries represented only 30 percent of Guangdong's output, with 13 percent under the control of central planners. Given the prominence of the entrepreneurial sector in China's export industries (Lardy claims they produce about one third of exports), there appeared to be a direct correlation between a market system and promotion of the foreign sector.

The changes in these three areas represent significant achievements in reforming China's Soviet-style economy that belie the frequent claims of retrogression in the post-Tiananmen period. However, there were continuing severe problems in three other areas of the economy that were, by and large, not addressed from 1989 to 1991. The first of these was localism. One manifestation was Guangdong's alleged resistance to the central government's efforts to curtail its special privileges.

Localism has, of course, been an endemic problem in China. During Mao's lifetime, county, city and provincial authorities acted like entrepreneurs, developing local industries, hampering movement of raw materials outside their jurisdiction and preventing goods produced elsewhere from entering. In the 1980s, efforts to weaken the central-planning bureaucracy only served to increase local power and, by so doing, to complicate further reform by creating redundant industrial lines which competed with the central government for everything from raw materials to energy and tax funds. A Communist party statement in November 1989 discussed reining in these local economies and creating stronger, central macroeconomic control. Yet, by late 1991 very little seemed to have been accomplished in this respect. Not only did local investment and protectionism continue unabated, but the central government was finding it more and more difficult to extract tax revenues from the localities. At a time of growing demands on its budget for infrastructural investment, subsidies, etc., the central government, from 1989 on, found itself confronted with declining revenues.

The Weak Center

Thus, the local autonomy that sustained reform in Guangdong could equally serve to inhibit national reform or, even worse, to promote disintegration into what one Chinese author has called "warlord economies." The fact that this province has been able to go its own entrepreneurial, outward-looking way reflects a weakness in the authority of the central government despite the rhetoric of post-Tiananmen. Without central authority, as embodied in a national tax and banking structure, any discussion of moving in the future from the old system of mandatory or direct planning to one of guidance or indirect planning is empty talk.

A second economic problem that remained unresolved in

the post-Tiananmen period is linked to this issue, namely the national deficit. With central government expenditures increasing, declining income due to a weak central tax structure was a particularly vexing problem. In the decade between 1981 and 1991 the deficit was said to have grown by 500 percent; between 1987 and 1991, it almost doubled. The major causes of this heavy burden were the largely unreformed condition of the state sector and the nation's price structure. Despite the movement on price reform described above, according to one report, between 10 percent and 15 percent of the government's income was still going toward the state subsidy on goods (mostly food items) sold to consumers at prices below cost.

However, the bulk of the deficit was the result of the drain on the budget caused by state enterprises. These 10,000 "large- and medium-sized enterprises" were the heart of the nation's economy. While they represented only about 3 percent of the nation's firms, they employed about two thirds of the urban work force and generated almost one half of the aggregate value of industrial output. Moreover, they not only employed most of the urban labor force. They were also the core of the nation's urban social welfare system, providing workers with everything from education to food to housing and medical care.

Although they had been given additional autonomy, these enterprises remained under the thumb of—and dependent upon—the old state-planning bureaucracy that determined what they produced and how they did so. These factories thus behaved more like bureaucratic offices than economic entities. They produced in response to instructions from higher up, with little sensitivity to market demand or profitability. Lacking such constraints—and kept afloat by government subsidies—most sustained inefficient production lines and bloated employment rolls. During the reform period of the 1980s, and particularly after June 1989, they were the slowest growing and the least profitable sector of the economy. In 1978, one quarter of the nation's state enterprises were showing a loss. By the end of 1991, figures in the Chinese press indicated that losing state firms had increased to one third (even in Guangdong!), one third of the remaining were breaking even and one third were turning a profit.

Despite reform proposals that would have allowed plant closings, they were kept in business. As loans were ignored, taxes left unpaid and unsold stockpiles grew, the state enterprises were given additional subsidies that came to represent 30 percent of the national budget. Despite this drain, little was done to reform them in the two years following June 1989. The government could not allow bulwarks of the national social security system to fail. Neither could it risk the social unrest that would result from paring down bloated employment rolls. For most Chinese workers, employment was a lifetime entitlement. The leadership would not chance disrupting the lives of two thirds of China's urban work force.

Agricultural Woes

Finally, there were the unresolved problems of China's most important economic sector—agriculture. Following the mid-1980s there had been signs that China's reform success story was in quiet crisis. There were difficulties maintaining the momentum of the first five years of reform that had produced a record harvest in 1984 and steadily rising rural incomes. After Tiananmen there were signs of stagnation in both areas. The reasons were complex. The manner in which the collectives had been broken up was partially responsible. For example, when collective land was allocated, individual families were given an average of 1.2 acres. In order to provide for equity in quality of land, these were divided up into as many as nine separate tracts. The efficiency of an agricultural system based on small scattered parcels was further undermined by the precipitous breakup of the collective structures that helped provide essential services, such as maintaining irrigation facilities, coordinating planting, etc. According to many observers, while the return to family farming was a crucial organizational step in increasing production, it had to be followed up by broad support from the central government, ranging from greater investment to stable sources of agricultural supplies.

Since the Tiananmen disaster, little has been done to address these problems. There was some talk of instituting a so-called two-tier system in agriculture that would complement the household-production system with collective or cooperative structures. However, the goals of such a system remained unclear and rural policy seemed to be a combination of ad hoc solutions and rhetoric. In order to eliminate some of the shortcomings of the contract system, the government returned to a system of set procurements, with bonuses for additional sales to the state. It also raised the state price paid to farmers for production and sought to increase the availability of less-expensive, state-supplied inputs. The result was that the agricultural system began to look like the urban economy where the existence of both a market and a strong state role not only created uncertain markets and sources of supply for inexperienced farmers, but worked to the advantage of better connected local cadres. These cadres could exploit official positions to impose arbitrary fees or to profit from the sale of state supplies. They could also abandon their political tasks and use their connections to profit in the growing private sector. Indeed, one survey showed that in 207 villages in wealthy Jiangsu province not one Communist party member had been recruited in the past decade.

The results of these agricultural policies were uneven. To be sure, in 1990 gross production exceeded the record of 1984. However, growth in China's population meant that per capita production actually declined. Moreover, rising inflation and an uncertain rural market structure had caused farmers' incomes to stagnate. Finally, the continuing state commitments to purchase goods at an inflated price and to sell at subsidized prices to the cities placed an additional burden on an already strained national budget. Although urban food prices were raised somewhat in early 1991, city dwellers were still benefiting at the expense of the treasury.

Shen Tong, a Tiananmen Square demonstrator, fled to the United States after the Chinese crackdown. Shen, shown leading a parade in honor of Martin Luther King Jr. in Atlanta, was arrested September 1, 1992, after returning to China for the first time in three years.

UPI/Bettmann

High subsidies remained the price paid by a regime seeking to avoid the urban unrest they feared would result from allowing agricultural products to be sold in the marketplace.

In sum, China's reform movement after the Tiananmen crisis presented a mixed picture. The predictions that reform was dead in China or that the clock would be turned back to the orthodox Marxist-Leninist-Stalinist-Maoist past were clearly wrong. Yet despite the continued progress in certain areas of reform, problems in fundamental sectors of the economy were not addressed. Reform momentum seemed to have slowed, with the post-Tiananmen leadership choosing to avoid some tough issues and to live with an inefficient, but stable, partially reformed economy.

Political Reform: Narrowed Boundaries and Lost Ground.
The demonstrations at Tiananmen and their aftermath posed two political challenges that China's leadership could not ignore. The first, of course, was to deal with the immediate situation. The second was to address the underlying causes of these events and to create both the political tone and structures that could provide the basis for the further development of communism in China.

The deployment of the army and the use of force against demonstrators were justified as acts of self-defense: they were necessary to protect the army and to preserve Chinese sovereignty and communism against foreign and domestic enemies. The brutal crackdown at Tiananmen Square lasted beyond the violence of June 3–4, however. Although Chinese officials spoke of leniency toward the majority of the demonstrators, they moved harshly against the leadership and those charged with violent acts. Many of the student leaders, bureaucrats and intellectuals were able to flee the country, but many were not and were arrested. By early 1991, only a few had stood trial in public. However, according to an April 1991 statement by the president of the Chinese Supreme Court, about 800 more had been tried in secret and apparently found guilty. In a few cases (*The Los Angeles Times* reported some 27) where the charge was violence—usually against nonstudents—the death penalty was imposed. The rest were assigned to labor camps or imprisoned under harsh conditions.

Within the government, the Communist party and society as a whole, institutions associated with promoting reform were either disbanded or placed under close surveillance. Important reform think-tanks staffed by allies of Zhao Ziyang, for example, were disbanded, and many of their leaders fled China. Curiously, the case of Zhao himself remained unsettled. Apparently Deng Xiaoping sought to avoid not only the signal that his purge might send abroad and to reform forces at home, but also a return to the bitter purges of the past.

China's leaders also took actions to prevent a recurrence of the Tiananmen demonstrations or what they perceived as developments similar to those in Eastern Europe and the Soviet Union. Interestingly, like Mao in his later years, many came to the conclusion that one of the principal reasons for the crisis of communism in China was the emphasis on economic construction at the expense of ideological transformation that had permitted the growth of such tendencies as "ultra-individualism" and "putting money above everything." China could avoid the fate of other Communist countries, they argued, only if ideological education became an essential element of building communism.

This meant, on the one hand, an emphasis on Deng's four cardinal principles. As Andrew Nathan of Columbia University has noted, these principles serve much the same function as the lines of a basketball court: they define the boundaries of permissible activity. In the years following the Tiananmen debacle, these boundaries shrank as the range of activities or speech considered antithetical to the Communist party, socialism in China, Marxist-Leninist-Maoist thought or the people's democratic dictatorship was broadened. As human-rights organizations in the West highlighted, those who strayed outside these boundaries were dealt with summarily—whether they were nonconforming intellectuals or Tibetans protesting in favor of greater cultural and political freedom. Reports of torture, solitary confinement and poor medical care all suggested the regime's determination to squash any signs of dissent.

Tightening Controls

Besides limiting the boundaries of permissible actions and dialogue, China's leaders also returned to ruling techniques of the past. Some of the levers of control—the military, Communist party ideology and public security—were strengthened. In addition there was a renewed emphasis on political study. In the years following the Tiananmen events, bureaucrats and workers throughout China took time off to study the essentials of "socialism with Chinese characteristics" or to take part in Communist education campaigns. Communist heroes deified during the Cultural Revolution were once again presented to the nation as models worthy of study.

There appeared to be other setbacks to the political reform agenda of the previous decade in the wake of the Tiananmen disturbances. The deployment of the military to restore order suggested that the army—or at least its top leaders—continued to play a crucial role in civilian politics. Similarly, the Communist party appeared to intervene more rather than less in day-to-day governing. China's elders called upon it once more to play its traditional roles of personnel supervisor and policy monitor.

With the Communist party playing a more dominant role, earlier attempts to raise the morale and quality of the state bureaucracy seemed problematic. The commitment to improve the quality of state cadres through the creation of a formal civil service that would replace the previous system of party appointments eroded, and the earlier glimmers of greater power for state representative bodies dimmed. Besides informal consultation with groups of the leadership's choosing, the major claim for the system's democratic nature lay in the resuscitation of officially sanctioned political parties. The administrative uncertainties caused by the post-Tiananmen retrenchment were exacerbated by problems that predated it. For example, it had been clear throughout the decade of the 1980s that attempts to streamline bloated bureaucracies were not succeeding. In late 1991, a Beijing radio report claimed that the number of administrative personnel had almost doubled since 1979, with one province reporting a tripling.

More seriously, the corruption that was so universally condemned in June 1989 apparently persisted. A Communist party career appeared to be less attractive for many of China's young people, and those who did opt to join saw membership as a way to enrich themselves through bribes and business connections. Although intended to highlight the government's efforts to eradicate such problems, frequent articles regarding the persistence of nepotism, bribe-taking or simple extortion all suggested that an honest bureaucracy had proven as elusive a goal as a streamlined one.

Post-Tiananmen reform evokes the economic austerity campaign that prevailed until late 1991. In politics, the leadership displayed the ability to bring society back under control and, as was the case with economics, to move back from the abyss. However, here the similarity ends. In contrast with economic reform that saw a general freeze on new policies, with negligible retrogression and some significant movement forward, political reform experienced a general freeze, with significant regression and negligible movement forward.

Reform Politics after Tiananmen. In China, the nature of reform politics proceeds from the Leninist assumption that political power flows downward from the small circle of leaders through a responsive bureaucracy to the citizenry. Deng Xiaoping and his colleagues have never really questioned the desirability of such a top-heavy decisionmaking process, seeing it as essential for effective and stable change. Although in a country as large and diverse as China, information and considerable political pressure certainly flow upward from bureaucracies and regions, elite politics have set the tone and direction of reform policies.

The reform coalition that began what was called China's second revolution in 1978 started to come apart in 1983–84. Some of the elite—most prominently Chen Yun—argued that reform had gone far enough and that it was time for a period of consolidation on some fronts and a halt on others. However, there were other leaders, among them Communist party head Hu Yaobang and Premier Zhao Ziyang, who argued for continued movement forward on both the economic and political fronts.

The first open break came in 1986–87 in response to student demonstrations in Beijing. Alarmed by the dangers of instability, the conservative elements (supported by Deng himself) bypassed party procedures and called a rump session of elders to force Hu's removal. This action by a group of aging party influentials marked a return to precisely the type of Maoist-era capricious and personalistic politics that Deng had sought to reform. By early 1987, reform seemed back on track. Deng threw his political support behind his remaining designated successor, Zhao Ziyang. When reform again ran into difficulties and the April 1989 demonstrations threatened stability, Deng cast his lot with the conservative forces once more, acceding to Zhao's removal—again by an irregular process.

With the Tiananmen incident, the reform of elite politics suffered another blow. The events of the summer of 1989 were both the culmination of and intensified the elite fragmentation and were the undoing of the efforts toward reforming politics at the top that had been developing since the mid-1980s.

The demonstrations, as well as the events taking place in the Soviet Union and Eastern Europe, had a chilling effect on the elite's commitment to reform. Although they spoke of foreign plotting, China's leaders were well aware that the events of the spring of 1989 were the inevitable results of the tensions and instabilities of reform. The near brush with disaster conditioned a much more cautious attitude—a sense that reform could be fatal for Chinese communism unless managed carefully, with an eye toward maintaining Communist party control and social stability.

This go-slow attitude toward reform was reinforced by the change in the configuration of power at the top after June 1989. Earlier there had been an influential group led by Zhao Ziyang that was ready to push forward rapidly with reform; a larger, more centrist group, associated with Premier Li, which while not opposed to reform argued for a slower pace and a narrower scope; and finally, a much smaller group of archconservatives that came to be associated with Chen Yun (and included Communist party elder Wang Zhen and party ideologist Deng Liqun) who counseled a halt to reform. The first group was discredited, leaving only the latter two. With Tiananmen, as David Shambaugh, lecturer in Chinese politics at the University of London, has noted, the center of politics in China, like that in the United States of President Ronald Reagan (1981–89) or in the Britain of Prime Minister Margaret Thatcher (1979–90), moved toward the conservative pole.

These were the leaders, chastened by their brush with turmoil, who took charge of the reform process in the months immediately after the Tiananmen incident. Their general concerns centered on the need to restore order while guarding against ideological erosion at home and subversion from abroad. To achieve these goals they imposed cultural restrictions, limited contacts with the West and generally slowed movement toward the development of a market economy.

Offsetting this conservative shift was the continuing presence of Deng Xiaoping. It has been said that reform in China is like riding a bicycle—you either go forward or you fall off. Events suggest that Deng subscribed to this view. In the fall of 1991 he was quoted as saying, "Don't be satisfied with the *status quo*. To bog down means regression." Thus, while his preoccupation with political stability left him with few doubts that the 1989 crackdown had been justified, over time Deng became increasingly concerned that post-Tiananmen factional alignments might threaten his economic reform program—and hence his place in history. Although he had resigned from his last formal Communist party post in the fall of 1989, Deng did not retire. The title bestowed upon him by the Western press, "China's paramount leader," was a recognition of his continuing role in the reform process. And, despite the blows that process suffered, Deng for the next three years strove to maintain its momentum.

Deng's Agenda

He did so in three ways. The first was by maintaining a close watch over personnel changes, particularly those at the top. Thus, in the summer of 1989, Deng intervened to assure the appointment of Jiang Zemin, the former Communist party chief of Shanghai, to succeed Zhao Ziyang as general secretary of the Communist party. Jiang had kept the peace in Shanghai during the spring of 1989 and had a reputation as a well-informed and pragmatic politician. Deng was seeking to position Jiang as a strong candidate to succeed him. In the spring of 1991, Deng again tried to buttress reform forces by sponsoring the promotion of the reformist Zhu

Rongji, former mayor of Shanghai, to a central government position. Finally, Deng also sought to limit the post-Tiananmen purges at the top levels of the party. He supported such moderate politicians as Li Ruihuan (whose more tolerant views on culture blunted the orthodoxy of Deng Liqun) and sought to avoid a witch-hunt at the highest levels by not only toning down the criticism of Zhao, but actually protecting him along with other pro-reform figures.

Secondly, Deng intervened at crucial junctures to see that reform policies were continued. In foreign policy, he maintained supervision over diplomatic affairs and economic matters, including China's opening to the outside world. According to reports from Hong Kong, it was his moderating influence that prevented Chinese conservatives from launching a Maoist-type ideological campaign against Soviet President Gorbachev. Domestically, he intervened to avoid further restrictions on cultural affairs and to protect crucial reforms such as increased use of the marketplace. Finally, there was evidence that Deng, sensitive to the pressures for continued reform coming from the export-oriented regions of China, sought to mobilize them in support of his efforts.

He was not unopposed in these efforts. Conservative figures intervened to promote their own allies and build support for their policies. They even resorted to factional tactics characteristic of the late-Mao period, using the media for thinly veiled attacks on opponents or for the promotion of policy lines. Most importantly, in much the same way as prevailed in the Maoist period, the attacks on many reform policies not only served to slow their implementation but also caused some bureaucrats to think twice about endorsing the reforms—an example of what the Chinese media have called the "fear of policy change."

The post-Tiananmen years demonstrated the crucial impact that top-level policymakers can have on the direction of reform. By the end of the 1980s, the unity of purpose and stable decisionmaking processes of the previous decade seemed lost. The upper levels of leadership were faction-ridden, with many Communist party leaders falling back on the tactics that characterized the bitter and divisive politics of the Maoist past. Personalism—the ability of individual leaders to exercise power and influence—remained a critical factor. Retired leaders continued to pull strings and hold rump meetings at crucial junctures. Such irregular procedures and elite carryings-on were, in large part, responsible for the inconsistent course of economic and political reform after 1989. Yet ironically, in the winter of 1991–92 the very personalism that seemed to inhibit reform made possible one more attempt at it. China's paramount leader, the 87-year-old Deng Xiaoping, intervened dramatically to break the political deadlock and end the post-Tiananmen policies of caution.

Reform Again

When Mao sought to redirect the course of Chinese politics, he was known to leave Beijing and visit organizations and areas whose policies he approved. In January 1992, Deng Xiaoping, accompanied by his daughter, made an inspection tour of the special economic zone of Shenzhen in bustling, reform-oriented Guangdong province, and the lesson was lost on few Chinese. He was placing his seal of approval on economic reform.

During the next month he visited three other economic reform sites and, at the end of February, the Central Committee issued a circular for national study summarizing his remarks and stressing "the necessity of seizing the present favorable opportunity to speed up the pace of reform and opening up and to concentrate energy on economic construction." By the summer of 1992, Deng's campaign had gained strength from an unusual March 1992 CCP politburo meeting and a dramatic meeting of the National People's Congress the same month. It was obvious that the outline of another reform thrust was beginning to emerge.

As Joseph Fewsmith of Boston University has noted, the factors which led Deng to take the initiative were rooted in both domestic and international politics. Ever since the Tiananmen crisis, he had been struggling to maintain the momentum of economic reform. By late 1991, the stabilization of the economy as well as the stark contrast between the failing Communist state enterprises and the thriving entrepreneurial sector provided propitious circumstances for a new initiative. More important, the constitution of the Communist party mandated that the 14th party congress be held in late 1992. This congress, probably the last to be held in Deng's lifetime, would establish the platform and choose the leaders for the next phase of the reform. With precongress maneuvering already begun, it was crucial that he take the initiative on both issues.

However, it was ultimately a foreign event—the abortive anti-Gorbachev coup of August 1991 and the subsequent demise of the Soviet system—that caused the political battle to be joined. In early September, conservative forces in Beijing seized upon the Soviet case as a prime example of "peaceful evolution." They argued that anti-Communist forces within the Soviet Union, encouraged by Western democratic nations, had succeeded in subverting the regime. Using rhetoric reminiscent of the last years of Mao, they issued statements about domestic class struggle and enemies within the Communist party. Not only did they call for increased emphasis on ideological training and greater care in choosing cadres, but, according to one Hong Kong report, Deng Liqun warned that "reform and opening up is itself a banner for peaceful evolution in China."

This was an obvious rebuke to Deng's reform platform that could not be ignored, particularly in the light of the forthcoming congress. Deng struck back by arguing that the lesson of the Soviet failure was that to ignore economic reform could only bring popular disaffection. Communism would not be saved by Cultural Revolution rhetoric, he maintained, but by reform that bettered the people's standard of living. In the period that followed, Deng pressed his offensive by a carefully orchestrated series of personal site visits and Communist party-state meetings that quickly came to reflect a changed political mood and the outline of what came to be called the "third wave" of reform.

According to the official version of his trip south, Deng set the new mood as follows:

> Reform and opening up require greater boldness and courageous experiments, and must not proceed like a woman with bound feet....The criterion for making a judgment should mainly be whether it is conducive to the development of the socialist productive forces, to the growth of the comprehensive national strength of the socialist state, and to the enhancement of the people's living standards [rather than whether it is labeled capitalist or socialist]....China must guard against rightism [subversion by the bourgeoisie], but should mainly guard against 'leftism'...which equates reform and opening to ushering in and developing capitalism....

This was a direct challenge to his reform opponents. It was apparently made even more explicit by positive references to Zhao Ziyang's pre-Tiananmen reform and by unpublished remarks to the effect that those who were not willing to promote reform should not hold office. In effect, Deng called for an end to preoccupation with ideological study and foreign subversion in favor of a new, primary emphasis on economic development. Individuals and policies would be judged solely on the basis of whether they contributed to that goal. As many observers have noted, it was entirely consistent with Deng's much-quoted quip in the 1960s that it made no difference whether a cat was black or white as long as it caught mice. Or, as one pro-Deng writer put it, measures that seemed to be capitalist in fact had no class nature and could be used by communism to develop the economy.

The impact of this changed tone was almost immediately apparent—indeed, some compared it to the mood after Mao's death. There was a reappearance of individuals whose earlier views had put them in disfavor. More importantly, the press came alive with discussions of economic reform and, over time, the outlines of specific policies emerged.

Many policies were not new, but they drew renewed impetus from Deng's call for boldness and his announcement that markets were not exclusively capitalist but rather could be used by a Communist system. Once again there was talk of "decreasing direct government administration over economic affairs [central planning] and enlarging the scope of indirect government macrocontrol" by means of fiscal and monetary tools. In line with this, there were renewed efforts at price reform; at the expansion of wholesale and futures markets, especially in agriculture; and at the expansion of securities markets in China. Similarly, as one might expect given Deng's trip to the special economic zones, there was a very strong emphasis on the foreign trade and investment sectors that by mid-1992 had resulted in as much foreign investment as in all of 1991. Localities were granted greater authority in dealing with foreign individuals and firms; changes were promised in regard to the extent to which Chinese regulations would be made public; and there was talk of adjusting exchange rates so as to move Chinese currency closer to convertibility. These policies were further evidence of China's continuing commitment to regain membership in the General Agreement on Tariffs and Trade (GATT), the 108-member institution seeking to force traders to follow the same rules.

Beyond these elaborations on earlier policies, there were hints of new economic-reform ground being broken. For example, in December 1991, so-called B shares in Chinese companies, which foreigners are permitted to buy, went on sale in the fledgling securities markets. Although the shares of only three companies could be bought, this was a startling reversal of policy. And, by the fall of 1992, not only had the numbers of such companies increased, but there were indications that foreigners might be allowed into previously "forbidden" sectors such as banking and insurance.

A major thrust of the third wave of reform seems to be

In the special economic zone of Shenzen, thousands lined up on August 18, 1992, to buy application forms for stock shares.

aimed at the most difficult and recalcitrant sector of the Chinese economy—the large state enterprises. At the end of 1991, the economic news from this sector was grim, as their losses increased and the revenues they turned over to the state shrank. What was even more striking was the continued contrast between their growth and that of other sectors: while state-owned industries grew 8 percent a year, the collective, private and foreign sectors grew 18 percent, 24 percent and 56 percent. Advocates of economic reform, including Deng Xiaoping, drew the obvious lesson: the orthodox Communist enterprises were operating at a disadvantage. They were restricted by higher tax burdens, an irrational price structure, the demands of mandatory state planning, limited decisionmaking powers, and the need to provide a wide range of social services to their workers. One commentary, which picturesquely depicted the nonstate enterprises as "monkeys" running free while the state industry "tigers" were tied down, argued that it was time to free the tigers.

This was precisely the thrust of the enterprise reform that

evolved during 1991–92. Its aim was not simply to free the tigers but to allow them to emulate the management and marketing techniques of the monkeys. Within the state enterprises, the object was to make both management and workers responsible for performance, and to give the former greater flexibility in dealing with the internal organization of the firm. This meant greater discretion in investment decisions and, most important, the right to fire redundant or inefficient laborers. Workers would no longer benefit from virtual lifetime employment or an income that bore little relation to the quality of their work. Their employment and payment, like that of management, would depend on their performance and that of the factory.

The place of the state enterprise within the broader economic system would also change. The new reforms were intended to force it to behave less like a bureaucratic arm of the state and more like an economic entity. Concretely this meant that most of the social-service functions of the factory would be phased out, and the enterprises could no longer count on large state subsidies if they generated losses. With the role of state planning reduced, these enterprises would be expected to enter the market and find their own sources of supply and customers. Failure to do so would bring bankruptcy—an almost unheard of eventuality. Finally, in order to further enhance such entrepreneurial behavior, there was talk of selling shares to workers or outsiders.

This initiative for state-enterprise reform, if successful, would radically restructure the Chinese economy. It is a dramatic example of the kind of boldness which Deng sought to elicit. However, what is even more striking is the contrast between the sweeping nature of the economic-reform initiative and the continuing narrow scope of political reform. In that area there seems to have been little change in Deng's thinking. While he seems willing to expose state enterprises to the marketplace, there is a continued reluctance to expose the Communist party or communism to political competition. Seeing an excessive emphasis on political reform as the cause of Gorbachev's failure, he continued his characteristic stress on the necessity of a stable, authoritarian political system. In April 1992 the official newspaper *People's Daily* quoted Deng as threatening that "as soon as elements of turmoil appear, we will not hesitate to take any means whatsoever to eliminate them as quickly as possible."

Thus, old political-reform themes prevailed amid the new rhetoric of bold economic experimentation. Reflecting the lessons of the Tiananmen demonstrations, there was strong talk—but perhaps less action—about punishing corrupt officials. In addition, there was continuing emphasis on the need to streamline the bureaucracy, curb waste and experiment with a civil service system. Moreover, despite talk of using indirect means to control the national economy, it was still unclear whether the center had created the political and fiscal tools to do so. Finally, while there was some relaxation in regard to cultural matters and ideological study, the boundaries formed by the four cardinal principles remained narrow. Despite Deng's warnings on the primary danger coming from the left, rightist or Western-oriented individuals and organizations were still carefully watched. Political reform continued to mean reform of the political structure to facilitate the smooth and honest operation of an authoritarian system dominated by the Communist party.

The months following Deng's initiative saw an intensification of political maneuvering. Both Deng and his political opponents sought to use internal channels and the public media to plead their cases. There were intensive lobbying efforts to gain political allies within the system. In particular, beginning in early 1992, political maneuvering centered on the preparations for the crucial 14th party congress as all sides struggled over the delegate list, the content of the Communist party program and the makeup of the party's central organs. The congress, which met October 12–19, reflected this conflict. Deng's contributions to the reform effort, as well as his slogan of "building a socialist market economy," were praised. However, there were also references to "peaceful evolution" and the need for "more-revolutionary" cadres. Similarly, although more-reform-minded cadres made significant gains, some more-conservative elements remained. Deng Xiaoping had unquestionably placed his mark on both the platform and personnel of the 14th party congress—but suggestions of inner-party differences persisted.

These political developments will surely have an impact on the future course of reform in China. To be successful, reform in Communist countries requires a united leadership, with effective political instruments at its disposal, prepared to move ahead with determination despite bureaucratic and popular resistance. In the early days of reform, the political environment came close to meeting these criteria. The environment since the Tiananmen crisis has been substantially different: a divided leadership faces considerable popular skepticism and holds uncertain control over a national bureaucracy of even more indeterminate reach or efficiency. This domestic political configuration will have a crucial impact on the future of the third wave of reform.

But it is not the only factor affecting the course of the reform movement. As Deng and his colleagues would be the first to acknowledge, international factors have a critical impact as well. Since its very inception, the reform movement has been deeply influenced by the perceptions of China and its place in the world that have been held not only by its own leaders but also by statesmen in other countries. Of particular importance, of course, have been the mutual perceptions of Beijing and Washington as well as the relationship which has been shaped by these views.

China's World:
Sino-Soviet-American Strategic Triangle

During much of the history of the People's Republic of China (PRC), established by the Communists in 1949, the "strategic triangle" of Sino-Soviet-American relations has had a crucial influence on that nation's foreign policy. In a post-World War II era decisively shaped by the confrontation between Moscow and Washington, China's policymakers were, more often than not, preoccupied with the question of how best to position the nation in response to the perceived threats or opportunities presented at each of the "corners" of this triangle.

In the fall of 1949, as "New China" prepared to declare the end of an era of victimization at the hands of international forces, the cold war had already begun. Acting on deep-seated feelings of affinity and admiration for Stalin's Soviet Union, China's new leaders aligned themselves with the Soviet bloc. With the outbreak of the Korean War in 1950, the subsequent Sino-American armed conflict, and the imposition of a Western economic embargo, China drew even closer to its Soviet allies. In the most dangerous days of the cold war, Beijing sought security and the means for economic development in what Mao Zedong called the "lean-to-one-side" policy.

However by the late 1950s and early 1960s, Mao himself came to doubt the wisdom of this approach. The American threat to China remained, but close ties with the Soviet Union seemed no longer to be the proper response. Rather, such ties complicated China's security problems as Soviet leader Khrushchev appeared ready to sacrifice Chinese needs in pursuit of "peaceful coexistence" with the West. On the economic front, Mao had concluded that despite the indispensable benefits of Soviet aid, the nation had to look for its own solutions to building communism. Economic assistance from abroad, he argued, allowed the penetration of foreign influences and undermined national self-confidence.

Tensions grew. By the mid-1960s, the Sino-Soviet alliance was a dead letter. In the years of the Cultural Revolution that followed, Maoist China turned its attention to the Third World, proclaiming itself the center of global revolution. Economic relationships with the rest of the world were kept at a minimum as the nation practiced the virtues of "self-reliance." China's diplomacy within the strategic triangle had shifted from reliance on the Soviet Union to offset the American threat to simultaneous opposition to both global superpowers.

It was soon apparent that this policy of dual confrontation had only worsened China's international position. To be sure, a Sino-American conflict had been averted in Vietnam during the mid-1960s. However, the Soviet threat was growing. In the wake of the 1968 invasion of Czechoslovakia and the Sino-Soviet border clashes of early 1969, the leadership in Beijing felt compelled to explore détente with the United States. The result was the secret trip of national security adviser Henry A. Kissinger to China in July 1971 and the visit of President Richard M. Nixon the following February.

The Sino-American détente of the early 1970s was classic

President Richard M. Nixon at a farewell banquet with Premier Zhou Enlai in February 1972 after they drew up the Shanghai communiqué committing their countries to normalize diplomatic relations.

balance-of-power politics within the triangular relationship that existed between the two countries and the Soviet Union. Mao sought a secure strategic position in which to achieve largely self-reliant economic development. Seeing China under Soviet threat, he operated on the principle that "my enemy's enemy is my friend." Deng Xiaoping, who, within two years of Mao's death in 1976, had emerged as China's paramount leader, saw the world somewhat differently. He and his colleagues seemed convinced that Mao's insistence on restricting economic and intellectual contacts with the outside world had done serious damage, costing China a decade or more of economic growth. To be sure, foreign penetration had to be monitored. However, the benefits to be reaped from trade, investment and cultural exchange were, they believed, too important to be ignored. After 1978, Deng and his colleagues involved the nation deeply in the global economy.

Still, the logic of the strategic triangle continued to shape

61

the nation's foreign policy. The cold war persisted and Mao's successors were also preoccupied with the Soviet military threat. They, too, sought to use alignment with the United States to assure a stable international environment within which the nation could focus on the more-interdependent economic growth. Indeed, during the late 1970s it seemed as if the alignment with Washington might extend to military cooperation or even a formal alliance.

In retrospect, the last years of President Jimmy Carter's Administration (1977–81) were the high point of the Sino-American strategic relationship. By the early 1980s, unhappiness with American policy, as well as a perception of a lessened Soviet threat, caused the Chinese to back away from any alignment with the United States. With the announcement that "China never attaches itself to any power or group of powers," the post-Mao leadership embarked upon what came to be known as an independent foreign policy. Talks with the Soviets were initiated and trade was increased. The strategic component of the relationship with the United States was downplayed while economic ties were promoted. The world, as seen from Beijing, had become less threatening.

However, just as China seemed to be cultivating this most advantageous position in the postwar strategic triangle, the global system began a transformation that would fundamentally change international politics for the first time in nearly four decades. In its early stages this transformation seemed quite beneficial to China. By the end of the 1980s, it seemed more threatening.

The Weakening of the Strategic Triangle

In March 1985, Gorbachev became the general secretary of the Communist party of the Soviet Union. During the next two years, he embarked upon a series of sweeping reforms in domestic and foreign policy. Although at first somewhat skeptical, by 1986 the Chinese leadership appears to have concluded that Gorbachev was a serious reformer and that his domestic success would result in a less aggressive Soviet foreign policy.

For a time it seemed that American belligerence would make such a Soviet readjustment difficult. However, in the Chinese view, President Reagan, under the combined pressures of the "Irangate" scandal, a rising budget deficit and the October 1987 stock market plunge, was—like Gorbachev—being compelled by domestic needs to ease international tensions. And as the superpowers negotiated such landmark decisions as the agreement to limit intermediate-range nuclear forces (INF), conciliatory Soviet gestures toward China proceeded apace. The Soviet Union agreed in April 1988 to pull its troops out of Afghanistan, announced its withdrawal from neighboring Mongolia in March 1989, and seemed to be pressuring Vietnam to pull its forces out of Cambodia, which Vietnam had invaded in 1978. By the end of 1988, Soviet and Chinese foreign ministers were beginning the first exchange of visits in 30 years and Gorbachev's trip to Beijing in the spring of 1989 was announced. There had not existed such a situation since 1949: China seemed to be enjoying stable and fruitful relations with *both* the United States and the Soviet Union.

And so it was possible for China's foreign policy to move beyond the nearly four decades of preoccupation with finding the proper posture in the conflict between the Soviet Union and the United States. The timing could not have been better. It appeared that China, in the midst of a historic restructuring of its Communist system, could look forward to a "long-term stable international environment in which…[to] focus its efforts on reform and modernization."

Although there were occasional Chinese criticisms of the inequality of a global economic system dominated by the developed nations and concerns regarding growing foreign influence, Beijing was rushing toward greater international economic involvement. By the end of 1988, its total foreign trade stood at $79 billion—more than two and a half times that of 1979. In the same year China signed $10 billion in foreign-loan agreements and almost 6,000 contracts for foreign investment valued at $5 billion. Its application for readmission to membership in GATT was pending and World Bank assistance to China had reached a high of nearly $2 billion. Finally, tens of thousands of Chinese were engaged in study and research abroad.

Of course, neither these policy shifts nor the more benign image of international affairs that motivated them were irreversible. From the perspective of Beijing, détente simply meant a lull in the Soviet-American rivalry. It could reignite. Tensions in other parts of the world persisted. More importantly, in China's view, the changed environment was not entirely beneficial for its interests. On the one hand, certain Chinese leaders were alarmed over the erosion of Communist values ("spiritual pollution" or "bourgeois liberalization") that accompanied greater exposure to Western ideas and technology. On the other, some observers of international affairs were worried about the impact that the demise of superpower rivalry might have on China's global importance. Would Beijing still be as actively courted if the strategic triangle were no more? How would China rank in a world in which economic power was a crucial determinant of international standing?

Global changes, as one Chinese commentator remarked, had "gone beyond the ability of traditional methods of inference or conventions to predict." Given the events that were to follow—global reactions to the Tiananmen crisis, the demise of the Soviet bloc and the dissolution of the Soviet Union—that was a gross understatement.

Defensive Diplomacy: China After Tiananmen

The spring 1989 demonstrations in Tiananmen Square were a media event witnessed by viewers throughout the world. Like a mixture of the Berkeley free-speech movement and Woodstock, the two-month rally in the heart of Beijing—which came to be known as the Beijing Spring—combined youthful fervor with idealism. When the Chinese army

President Mikhail S. Gorbachev is greeted on May 15, 1989, by a Chinese honor guard as he arrives for the first Sino-Soviet summit in 30 years. The historic event was overshadowed by massive pro-democracy demonstrations.

Reuters/Bettmann Newsphotos

moved in to crush the movement, enthusiasm turned to revulsion and then to indignation.

Many Western governments expressed their anger and took concrete steps to punish China. Outrage was especially strong in the United States, particularly on Capitol Hill. Other nations also took actions: Switzerland canceled arms sales, Germany froze $110 million in development funds, and Canada withdrew from three development projects. Sino-French relations particularly suffered when Paris gave asylum to some of the principal leaders of the Tiananmen demonstrations. Though more restrained, Japan went along with the censuring statement by the Group of Seven (G-7) major industrialized nations and suspended 14 aid projects while delaying the implementation of its 1990–94 aid package to China. Finally, international organizations such as the World Bank and the Asian Development Bank expressed their displeasure with China by suspending projects.

Most interesting was the Soviet reaction. While he was in

Beijing for the May summit, Gorbachev was circumspect in his reactions to the events in Tiananmen Square. Despite the fact that his reforming zeal seemed to have captured the imagination of many demonstrators, the Soviet leader was careful not to offend his hosts. When the military suppression took place, Gorbachev, who had suffered politically from the earlier violence in the Georgian republic, had no choice but to allow his spokesman to depict the Soviet leadership as "extremely dismayed" at the use of force. However, the Kremlin also strongly criticized those in the West who imposed sanctions and welcomed the Chinese foreign minister to Moscow. Gorbachev was clearly seeking to maintain the momentum of the recent summit.

For the Chinese leadership, the economic and political sanctions, as well as the vocal condemnations of their actions, posed a major challenge. True, Deng and his colleagues could note that fewer than 20 percent of the countries with which China had relations had actually criticized Beijing's actions. However, those who did were major powers whose attitudes would shape the decisions of international organizations as well as private business people.

In devising a diplomatic response to these developments, China's policymakers reverted to old ways of viewing the world. One of these, drawn from the Cultural Revolution period, emphasized the dangers of anti-Communist collusion between subversive elements at home and abroad. It was argued after Tiananmen that this so-called counterrevolutionary riot had resulted from the actions of "a few conspirators" in the Communist party who "colluded with hostile anti-Communist and antisocialist forces in Western countries... [to] establish a Western bourgeois republic...."

Other instinctive outlooks had their roots in earlier history, drawing on the cold-war period of the 1940s and 1950s. Chinese statements during the summer of 1989 characterized contemporary Western actions as extensions of the policies of American secretaries of state Dean Acheson and John Foster Dulles. Having failed to overthrow Communist regimes with military force, they and their contemporary successors pursued a policy of "peaceful evolution." Through the use of cultural-exchange programs, propaganda activities such as those of the Voice of America, and economic assistance, they sought to nourish subversive elements within Communist nations. This was what came to be known as "smokeless war."

Western Ideology Threatens

The evolution of a benign worldview was suddenly arrested. China's world had not seemed as threatening since the early 1970s—although the nature of the threat had significantly changed. The earlier military threat had been replaced by an intensified ideological threat from the West. And, like Mao before them, many Chinese leaders warned that a global class struggle against bourgeois ideology was necessary to protect the integrity of Chinese communism. This was, as one authoritative journal put it, the "new cold war."

While some in China's top echelons, led by antireform figures like Wang Zhen and Deng Liqun, emphasized the previously discredited Maoist rhetoric of international class struggle and ideological subversion, there was no return to Mao's foreign policies. For example, there was no attempt to revive the close Sino-Soviet alliance of the 1950s. Indeed, many of China's older leaders watched in horror as the states of Eastern Europe, with the apparent support of Gorbachev, abandoned communism. The Soviet leader soon came to be viewed in Beijing as a subversive force. A businesslike Sino-Soviet relationship was sustained, but some more-conservative Chinese leaders pressed for a rekindling of the ideological polemics of the Khrushchev era.

Neither would there be a return to Maoist policies of economic isolation or confrontation with those powers which opposed China. In the months after the Tiananmen Square crisis, some more-conservative Chinese leaders may have argued for a limiting of contacts with the West. However, Deng

67

Xiaoping himself took every occasion to stress that China's economic opening to the world would continue. Although at home one heard the Marxist rhetoric of class struggle, abroad Chinese diplomats used the well-established and universal principle of national sovereignty to defend their actions. China, Deng argued, would brook no foreign interference in the management of its domestic relations, but it would not be provocative. Diplomats and business people who respected China's sovereignty would be warmly welcomed in Beijing. As for the others, Deng counseled patience: he confidently predicted that they would eventually change their view if the nation remained stable. In the end, his more moderate approach prevailed.

Thus, Chinese foreign policy in the year following the Tiananmen demonstrations was one of damage control in a threatening international environment characterized by sharp reactions to the events of June 3–4 and the perception in Beijing of a renewed capitalist ideological campaign stimulated by the failures of communism in the Soviet Union and Eastern Europe. The results of this foreign policy were mixed. On the negative side, tourism and trade fell off; most foreign lending was frozen, and China's credibility was seriously damaged. On the positive side, most of the mechanisms for China's political and economic integration into the world remained in place. Indeed, in 1990 the United States once again granted Beijing most-favored-nation (MFN) status, which meant Chinese exports were elegible for the lowest U.S. tariffs. Some nations, particularly among China's Asian neighbors, actually increased their trade and investment in China.

Looking back over the year following the Tiananmen Square crackdown, Deng and his colleagues could thus feel some satisfaction. Although they had made occasional concessions to world public opinion, such as the suspension of martial law in Tibet and Beijing, as well as the release of some dissidents, China had held its ground in the face of enormous global pressure. In the summer of 1990, one official journal drew the following conclusion from the events of the past year: "China cannot do without the world, neither can the world do without China." It may well have been this minimal confidence that, according to a Hong Kong source, prompted the Communist party foreign policy group to recommend replacing the reactive foreign policy that had prevailed since the Tiananmen Square crisis with one that took the initiative in foreign affairs.

Beijing's Diplomatic Offensive

From April to August 1990, Beijing moved on several fronts to court world opinion. Important new laws were announced that liberalized regulations and increased opportunities pertaining to foreign investment. Personal diplomacy was expanded as Premier Li Peng visited the Soviet Union and President Yang Shangkun made a tour of several Latin American countries—the first by a Chinese head of state. Important diplomatic victories were scored when relations were established with Saudi Arabia and it was announced that they would soon be established with Singapore and restored with Indonesia. Finally, China even seemed to make some concessions to world opinion—and in exchange for the granting of MFN—when it allowed the dissident astrophysicist Fang Lizhi and his wife to leave their refuge in the American embassy in Beijing for Britain.

By July, there was evidence of a slight crack in the economic sanctions against China. At the Houston, Texas, G-7 meeting, Prime Minister Toshiki Kaifu told his colleagues that Japan, always a reluctant participant in the sanctions, would resume lending to China. Whether this would have been the beginning of a more general breakdown of post-Tiananmen sanctions, as some Chinese have argued, is difficult to determine because the world situation changed dramatically in August when Iraq invaded Kuwait. In the escalating crisis that preceded Operation Desert Storm, and even in its aftermath, China skillfully used its increased visibility and prestige to accelerate the momentum of its post-Tiananmen diplomatic comeback.

China's greatest diplomatic asset was its position as one of the five permanent members (along with France, Russia, Britain and the United States) of the Security Council of the United Nations—the body which spearheaded the response to Iraq. Because a Chinese veto could frustrate attempts to give the response an international coloration, the nation was not only catapulted back into the global spotlight, it became the object of intense diplomatic courtship by many who had sought to punish it after the Tiananmen crackdown. China's new importance yielded almost immediate diplomatic fruits. In late 1990 the World Bank and the Asian Development Bank resumed their lending; the European Community dropped its sanctions; and President George Bush entertained China's foreign minister Qian Qichen at the White House.

Throughout the next year, China's diplomatic momentum gained speed. By early 1992, the Japanese and British prime ministers, the Italian premier and the American secretary of state had all visited China, suggesting that most of the ties damaged by the Tiananmen crisis were in the process of being repaired. Beyond this, a successful trip by Premier Li Peng to India, China's role in the settlement of the Cambodian conflict, the establishment of diplomatic relations with Israel, and the normalization of relations with the Socialist Republic of Vietnam all constituted major diplomatic breakthroughs.

The specter of a post-Tiananmen-crisis China, isolated or shunned by the world, thus never really materialized. Beijing's diplomatic line of yielding only marginally to external pressure while maintaining openness to the international system seemed to have paid off handsomely—and Deng and his colleagues used this success to bolster the regime's position at home. China's diplomatic victories, the nation was told, were the result of the political stability that had followed the "turmoil" of Tiananmen Square. A "new situation" in the world favorable to reform and the building of communism in China had developed. Indeed, not only was China's strategic environment more benign than it had been in more than four decades, but economic ties with the world were accelerating. The Chinese government reported that foreign trade in 1991 had grown by nearly 18 percent and the value of foreign investment contracts by 68 percent over the previous year.

Yet, despite this apparent confidence, the leadership still perceived Chinese communism as developing in a world which one commentator characterized as "turbulent and unstable" because of the rapid changes of 1991–92. The fundamental cause was the denouement of a process that Beijing had seen developing in the late 1980s—the weakening of the U.S.S.R. and the emergence of the United States as the world's sole superpower.

Impact of Soviet Disintegration

The Soviet Union's rapid decline caught Beijing as unawares as it did the rest of the world. Although there were rumors that conservative forces in Beijing were cultivating hard-line groups within the Soviet leadership and that only Deng's intervention had prevented a Chinese statement of support for the anti-Gorbachev plotters, the attempted coup of August 1991 complicated China's situation. On the one hand, the nation's strategic position was enormously enhanced: it no longer had to contend with a military superpower on its borders and there were reports that China would strengthen its own military through purchases from Soviet stocks. Moreover, geographic proximity and economic complementarity contributed to growing trade with the states of the former Soviet Union.

On the other hand, although China promptly recognized the independent republics that succeeded the Soviet Union, it did not wholeheartedly welcome their emergence. The Soviet Union's collapse was a grievous blow to Marxism-Leninism that added to China's isolation in a globe that was swept by a "democratic revolution," and weakened the regime domestically by undermining its claims about the superiority of Communist ideology. Finally, the existence of independent Islamic republics on the borders where China's own, sometimes restive, Muslim population lives raised security concerns.

The most serious consequence of the demise of the Soviet Union was its impact on the pattern of world politics. Chinese officialdom declared that this event had finally and decisively ended the bipolar cold-war world. An unbalanced multipolar system in which power shifted to the developed capitalist countries—Western European nations, Japan and the United States—was emerging. Indeed, one Chinese commentator called the relations between these nations the new triangle in world affairs.

Like the previous Sino-Soviet-American triangle, the pattern of interaction between these nations combined cooperation with conflict. In the Chinese view, their cooperation centered around creating an interdependent global economic system designed to promote their common, capitalist growth. In addition, they shared the desire to dominate this global economy and, of equal importance to the Chinese, a determination to "spread their social system, political and economic formulas, ideologies, and value concepts throughout the world." The major conflict in the triangle, as Beijing commentators saw it, was the resistance of Japan and Europe to America's attempt to play the role of hegemonic power. The Japanese and Europeans preferred to share equally with the United States in the dominance of the world.

In this tripolar struggle, the United States was seen as having a temporary advantage, based on its military prowess and technological strength. However, as one Chinese commentator put it, there was a "mismatch between its [the American] ambition for global hegemony and its ability...." In the post-cold-war struggle, "comprehensive national strength" included not simply military might but also economic and technological power. In pursuit of such national power, the capitalist competitors of the United States were not simply working to keep Washington out of the European and Asian markets. They were also striving to develop their economic and technological capabilities in order to overtake the United States. Indeed, one journal close to the Chinese Ministry of Foreign Affairs noted that "Japan's economic strength has replaced the Soviet Union's military strength as the main threat against the United States."

This Chinese version of the new international order that developed in late 1991 and 1992 had evolved from the key premises of the worldview that had emerged in the late 1980s: the trend toward a multipolar world, the importance of dialogue and the possibility of tension giving way to détente. However, it was clear from Chinese commentaries and the statements of its leaders that they perceived this post-cold-war world as *more* dangerous than that of the earlier period.

Resistance to Western Democratic Values

The first threat was in the ideological sphere. Ever since the Tiananmen Square demonstrations, the Chinese leadership had been more sensitive to the impact of "subversive" foreign ideas that filtered in as a result of the economic open-door policy, cultural exchanges, study abroad, etc. The concept of "peaceful evolution" that had emerged in the summer of 1989 was the leaders' way of characterizing the threat. By late 1991, the danger appeared even graver to some more-conservative Chinese leaders. The capitalist developed nations led by the United States, riding the crest of self-confidence born of the failure of communism in Eastern Europe and the Soviet Union, had become more aggressive in their insistence that Western democratic values be the conceptual basis for the new world order. As a result, foreign ideas could be expected to intrude even more on China, and its human-rights record was bound to come under closer scrutiny.

A second threat emanated from the importance of economic and technological prowess in forming the basis of diplomatic influence. In the past, China's global influence had derived from largely intangible factors—including its strategic position in the Pacific and in the Sino-Soviet-American triangle. With the end of the cold war and the relaxation of military tensions, such intangibles counted for far less than economic and technological strength—areas in which China was most deficient. Even worse, the only way China could develop these strengths—and empower the nation—was through participation in the interdependent world economic system via the import of technology, the promotion of foreign investment, the development of export-oriented industry and foreign borrowing. Given the logic of the Chinese leadership, this empowerment could only come at a price. China would not only risk the intrusion of foreign ideas but also its entanglement in an international economic system over which the nation might have very little control. It was a classic catch-22 situation. And as China's leaders sought to develop an appropriate foreign policy response during 1991–92, the contradictions became apparent. What resulted was not only a policy that often seemed longer on rhetoric than on realistic solutions, but one which reflected serious divisions within the leadership.

The rhetoric was most apparent in the Chinese version of the new world order. The tripolar world of the post-cold-war era, it was argued, was just another version of previous hegemonic systems where one or more nations had dominated. A truly *new* international order would have to be created that would allow for genuine multipolarity as well as equality among nations and take the principles of national sovereignty and noninterference in domestic affairs for its doctrinal basis. Specifically (and with an eye to the human-rights issue), such an order "would respect the right of each country to choose any political system or economic structure to suit its own national condition." Finally, it should be complemented by a "new economic order" that would protect the interests of the developing countries.

Delving back into the history of their own diplomacy, China's leaders suggested that the Five Principles of Peaceful

Coexistence that emerged during the 1950s might be the basis for such an order. As several scholars have noted, Beijing's insistence on the all-importance of nation-state sovereignty might be losing relevance in an increasingly interdependent world, but for a beleaguered Chinese leadership it is anything but irrelevant.

China's foreign policy has been more than rhetoric, however. In 1991–92, several heads of state of major nations visited Beijing, and Chinese leaders were visiting countries from Thailand to Switzerland to Mongolia. Special efforts were made closer to home to strengthen economic and political ties with Asia. These efforts have been intensified. In regard to Hong Kong, China has made considerable progress in establishing a strong economic and political presence in preparation for regaining title to the colony in 1997.

In addition, China's ties have rapidly developed with the Central Asian successor-states to the Soviet Union. Moreover, despite the complications posed by its close relations with North Korea, ties with South Korea have grown since Tiananmen, with two-way trade reaching nearly $6 billion in 1991, and the two nations have established diplomatic relations. Finally, the first-ever meeting between a Chinese Communist party leader and the emperor of Japan in April 1992, as well as the visit to China by the emperor the following October, highlighted the growing importance of ties to a country that is China's leading trading partner and provider of low-interest loans.

Interdependence and Independence Go Hand in Hand

Such expanded diplomacy was consistent with the important place that national sovereignty occupied in the Chinese view of the world. However, numerous Chinese commentators on foreign affairs have noted that insistence on national independence might be a costly luxury for late-developing nations which, on their own, can neither protect their interests nor strengthen their economies. Only by welcoming foreign investment and participating in international organizations that are genuinely multilateral can such protection and economic advancement be achieved. Interdependence and independence are complementary rather than contradictory concepts.

It is against this background that the new efforts to increase foreign investment and trade have taken place. Moreover China has also actively promoted—and been part of—regional and international multinational organizations. Not only has Beijing advocated a strengthened (but restructured) UN, but it continues to seek membership in GATT and to benefit from the assistance of such bodies as the World Bank. In Asia, China is promoting cooperation on many levels, ranging from increased borrowings from the Asian Development Bank to its sponsorship of a Sino-Soviet-North Korean project in the Tumen river delta (dubbed the Rotterdam of the Far East), its active participation (alongside Taiwan) in the Asia-Pacific Economic Cooperation Council and its April 1992 hosting of the UN's Economic and Social Commission for Asia and the Pacific.

There is much to support the contention frequently made by Chinese commentators that the global and regional environment today is the most favorable for China's domestic development since 1949. There are few security concerns and economic involvement appears to be growing. There are also problems.

Sino-American relations are at one of their lowest points since the Nixon visit in 1972. In addition, its neighbors still approach China cautiously, particularly in light of recent evidence of a strengthening of Beijing's military muscle. There remain unsettled territorial issues with Japan, Vietnam and the nations of the former Soviet Union. Indeed, distrust of Beijing increased when, in early 1992, the National People's Congress approved legislation asserting Chinese sovereignty over a number of disputed islands in the region and approved American oil exploration in a disputed area of the South China Sea. Lastly, there is the continuing ambivalence in relations with Japan. The memories of the 1930s and

1940s are still very much alive in China. Although the cultivation of economic and political ties with Japan is an important aspect of the strategy to achieve accelerated development, there is still concern that the nation may fall victim to growing Japanese economic and political dominance in the region.

China's ties with international organizations are also not without problems. When the five permanent members of the Security Council met in New York in January 1992, China's Li Peng seemed very much the odd man out. It was not simply that he was associated with the brutality at Tiananmen. China's rhetoric seemed out of step with that of the other major powers. In addition, foreign investment and participation in international organizations court the danger of infringement on China's prized sovereignty. The growing integration of the Chinese economy with the rest of Asia raises the danger that national unity might be threatened as parts of the country—particularly the south—reinforce their localist tendencies by strengthening international economic links. Moreover, in order to gain membership in GATT or to obtain World Bank loans, China must recast some of its practices or permit scrutiny of its economy.

There is, on the one hand, a growing recognition that survival in the post-cold-war world requires accelerated development that, in turn, necessitates greater integration into the global economy. On the other hand, China's leaders seem aware that they must compromise some of their sovereignty in doing so and that they are approaching integration from a position of vulnerability. As China enters the 1990s it is by no means clear how its leaders will be able to achieve the benefits of both independence and interdependence.

The World After Tiananmen and into the 1990s

The impact of the Tiananmen crisis on China's international environment has not been as uncomplicated as pundits predicted during the summer of 1989. China has not become a global outcast. To be sure, fortuitous events such as the Persian Gulf war contributed to this outcome, but credit must also be given to the skillful—and flexible—diplomacy of China's so-called hard-line leaders. In fact, judging from such tangible indicators as foreign trade and investment and diplomatic activity, the nation has regained much of the ground lost in the summer of 1989. Indeed, it may even be in a somewhat better position than it was at that time.

However, tangible indicators alone yield a very partial picture of the impact of Tiananmen Square events on both the way that much of the world views China and the way China's leaders view the world. The vivid and ugly images of troops crushing youthful demonstrators shattered the widely held belief outside of China that the nation was inexorably marching down the road to peaceful reform. As a result, while foreign corporations and individuals continue to invest, they do so with much greater chariness of the risks involved. Similarly, the uncertainty about China's future has clouded the return of the British colony of Hong Kong in 1997 and reunification efforts with the Nationalist government on Taiwan. In the former case, concern over Chinese intentions has generated increased middle-class demands for greater self-rule before the British colony becomes a part of China in 1997. As for Taiwan, although economic relations with the mainland continue to grow, the disturbances of 1989 not only called into question promises of fair treatment for the island should it rejoin China but increased the confidence of many that the comparative stability of the island makes such a move unnecessary.

Similarly while world events such as the Gulf war have benefited China's image abroad, others, such as the demise of communism in Eastern Europe and the Soviet Union, have hurt it, particularly in regard to its relations with Western Europe and the United States. As the Berlin Wall came down and "the democratic tide" swept Eastern Europe and the Soviet Union, China seemed to be swimming against a global wave of change. As a result, many statesmen tended to be more critical of China, and there were signs of a shift of investment interest away from the nation and toward the former Communist states of Eastern Europe and the Soviet Union.

Ambivalence Predominates

It is clear that these very same events have had an enormous impact on the way that China's leaders look at the post-Tiananmen world. Prior to the summer of 1989, there had been occasional concerns voiced regarding the dangers of foreign subversion. However, the Chinese leadership seemed to continue to view the world as increasingly benign and to rush headlong into global economic interdependence. Since that summer, their policies and attitudes have become far more ambivalent. Although they have maintained much of the policy and rhetoric of the opening-up process, the words and actions of China's leaders belie a much-enhanced sense of threat emanating from global economic and ideological currents.

In part, this uncertainty reflected the leadership's *shared* sense of the complications posed by the post-cold-war world. They *all* appeared to perceive the dangers of seeking interdependence while preserving national sovereignty. However, the ambivalent policy is also due to the fact that groups within the leadership have tended to weigh differently the dangers confronting China.

Throughout the post-Tiananmen period (and particularly after the dissolution of the Soviet Union) the more antireform elements within the leadership, such as Chen Yun and Wang Zhen, have attempted to use the threat of "peaceful evolution" to limit the opening to the outside world and to promote with great vigor a "socialist education movement" at home—even, or perhaps particularly, if it meant slowing the course of economic reform. Chinese communism, they believed, could only survive by protecting itself from the contamination of foreign ideas and reinvigorating the Communist ethos of the population.

Deng Xiaoping, on the other hand, while no less concerned about the ideological and economic dangers of increased global involvement, seems convinced that China must take the risk if it is to have the technology needed to survive in a new world. In the post-Tiananmen period he has consistently tried to temper the warnings against "peaceful evolution" with calls to continue the open door. During the months that followed the failed Soviet coup of August 1991, it was his decisive intervention that blunted the efforts of more-conservative elements to present a more-belligerent face to the world and limit the scope of global involvement. Under his prodding, China has opened its economic door *even wider* to the world and has maintained its vigorous diplomatic campaign.

The impact of Tiananmen on China's global position has been much more subtle than that posited by the conventional wisdom that developed during the summer of 1989. China has not been excluded from the world nor has it chosen to withdraw. However, developments at home and abroad have clearly shaken the leaders' confidence in their ability to deal with the world. They have divided the leadership and rekindled a debate that has preoccupied Chinese statesmen since the end of the nineteenth century: How best to benefit from a world system whose values and economic structure threaten the very integrity of the nation.

Much of the dramatic deterioration in Sino-American relations can be attributed to the fact that policymakers in both Washington and Beijing have come to view each other through lenses decisively shaped by their respective images of the nature of China's post-Tiananmen reform and the evolution of the post-cold-war world.

Sino-American Relations

In May 1991, a Hong Kong newspaper reported that China's foreign minister, Qian Qichen, had remarked in private that before the Tiananmen Square protests, the United States and China had fundamentally misperceived each other. China saw Washington as a dependable partner whose capitalist system had undergone change, while America's policymakers perceived China as moving toward capitalism. It is immaterial whether Qian actually made this statement. What is important is that it could have been made at any point during the last century. Mutual misperceptions or clouded understandings are the stuff of which Sino-American relations have always been made.

The American view, characterized as misinformed "scratches on our minds" by political scientist Harold R. Isaacs, has been an ambivalent one, combining both deep suspicion and paternalistic concern. In this environment, some missionaries were drawn by the prospect of millions of souls to be saved. Businessmen were attracted by the allure of a huge market—"If every Chinese bought only one straight pin...." Finally, educators and educational institutions arrived to establish a large number of hospitals, schools, exchange programs, etc. All sought, however, to change China in their image—or, more precisely, their interests. Most became disillusioned and fell back on the more sinister stereotypes when the nation failed to meet their expectations. World War II sympathy for China turned to fear of the Chinese "fighting hoards" during the Korean War, and fear turned to fascination after the Nixon visit in 1972.

Of course, sentimentality supposedly had little to do with the Kissinger-Nixon design. Policy was firmly based on the importance of alignment with China for American global interests. Still, Nixon's view of China seemed the epitome of the uncertain American image, suggesting that traces of ambivalence even remained in the minds of those within government. It was just obscured by the diplomatic priorities of the day.

There has been much uncertainty on the China side, as well. As Professor Shambaugh has noted, the Chinese phrase for American imperialism, *Mei diguo zhuyi*, literally translates as beautiful imperialism—an oxymoron, perhaps, but one which well captures the view that many Chinese have had of the United States over the past century. In the early twentieth century, many intellectuals thought "science" and "democracy" would be keys to China's salvation. The beauty of America lay precisely in the way in which its political institutions and economy represented, for these individuals, the highest development of these values. Although decades of Communist propaganda sought to undermine this image of the United States, it has had remarkable resilience. Indeed, in the summer before the Tiananmen disturbance, many officials were outraged by a television series entitled *River Elegy* that argued bluntly that Chinese culture had exhausted its potential. The only alternative was to look to the West and, in particular, to a very idealized United States.

Despite the attraction of Western values, it was not that easy for Chinese intellectuals to abandon their own heritage—and identity. More than one have shifted back and forth during their lifetimes, sometimes decrying, sometimes praising American values. The major reason for this fluctuation lay in the "imperialist" side of the United States. As Mao once wrote, those who had "fond dreams" of learning from the West were confronted with the difficult question: "Why were the teachers always committing aggression against their pupil?" At crucial junctures, even seemingly pro-American intellectuals turned against the United States when it appeared to have acted in such a way as to harm China's interests.

Mao and his successors have frequently demonstrated distrust for China's intellectuals, even as they have tried to exploit their anti-American feelings. However, it is also true that many of China's leaders have harbored similar feelings, admiring the accomplishments of American capitalism, on the one hand, while they bitterly condemn its policies toward China and the world, on the other.

Relationship Seems Stabilized

This was the historical basis of the Sino-American relationship that developed in the decade after the normalization of relations in 1978. With the Soviet threat perceived as immediate and the West—particularly the United States—eager to provide technology and education, Beijing cultivated the relationship. To be sure there were periodic concerns regarding "bourgeois liberalization" or the "flies" of Western values that might get through China's open door. However, these worries were swept under the rug, along with U.S. concerns regarding such issues as human and reproductive rights, the future of Taiwan and Hong Kong or the serious difficulties of doing business in China. Until the summer of 1989, American imperialism seemed more beautiful than not and China seemed to be, at last, "becoming like us." A century of ambivalence seemed to have been put to rest on both sides of the Pacific.

The Tiananmen Square crisis demonstrated that this was

not the case. Instead, Sino-American relations were launched on one more swing toward hostility. The immediate—and indirect—cause was the April to June demonstrations and their aftermath. But there were also global contributing factors: the end of the cold war, the dissolution of the Soviet Union and the emergence of the United States as the single global superpower.

The result of this confluence of factors was that problems that in the past might have been settled congenially or even finessed became difficult issues that contributed to an atmosphere of almost constant crisis—and at times, near rupture—in relations. Considering the range of issues that came to divide the two countries and the intensity with which they have done so, it seems remarkable that Sino-American relations have been able to make it through these turbulent years.

The Strategic Dimension

The foundation of the Sino-American relationship throughout the 1970s and most of the 1980s was a common opposition to the Soviet Union. This priority was so high on the list for both countries that it moved leaders in Washington and Beijing to paper over other potential rifts. Although the strength of this strategic factor was waning by the end of the 1980s, its demise was the result of developments in the Soviet Union. The overarching sense of purpose for the relationship, and thus its major bonding force, evaporated just as relations were plunged into crisis as a result of Tiananmen.

This is not to say that Beijing pursued policies consistently inimical to the United States or became unimportant. The very fact of China—a country of well over one billion occupying a large landmass in Asia—makes it an important strategic factor in Washington's calculations for the post-cold-war world. History has shown that American isolation or slighting of China has inevitably damaged U.S. strategic interests. Moreover, in the current world, China has shown its strategic worth in specific diplomatic circumstances. For example, the Persian Gulf war demonstrated that its cooperation as a permanent member of the UN Security Council was essential. Moreover, during the fall of 1991, China played a crucial role as backer of the Khmer Rouge in the brokered peace in Cambodia and has been a critical intermediary in dealing with the often unpredictable, and inaccessible, regime in North Korea. Finally, Beijing's recognition of Israel as well as its greater involvement in the Middle East peace process also would seem to highlight its strategic importance to the United States.

Still there is much that divides the two nations. China and the United States have sharply diverging views of the place that each occupies in the new world order. China's support for Burma and Iran and Chinese arms sales have been growing areas of contention. China is an important provider of conventional arms to Third World countries, earning foreign exchange ($300 million in 1991) in the process. It is alleged to have provided nuclear technologies to Algeria and Pakistan. Finally, the sighting of Chinese solid-fuel missile launchers in Pakistan and persistent rumors of possible contracts for the sale of nuclear and missile technologies to Libya, Iran, Iraq, Syria and Pakistan have caused concern in both the Congress and the White House.

Negotiations with the Chinese on this issue have been difficult, and neither side has been satisfied with the manner in which they have proceeded. As with human rights, Beijing has been quick to argue that China is being held to standards quite different from those of Western countries that more actively engage in arms sales. Still, in February 1992, China agreed to abide by international guidelines on sales of missile technology to the Middle East in exchange for Washington allowing the sale of certain high-technology items to China. Nonetheless, many in Washington (particularly in Congress) remained suspicious, noting previous failures on the part of Beijing to honor similar commitments.

How one views the strategic relationship between the

United States and China is almost a classic instance of the bottle half full or half empty. Some China-watchers, such as former Carter Administration aide Michel Oksenberg, would argue that while the nature of the strategic relationship has changed, China remains an important international actor, crucial to American objectives in Asia and the world. Despite deep differences and Chinese rhetoric, there are sufficient reasons to nurture relations and sufficient grounds for agreement between the two countries. Others, such as former State Department official Roger Sullivan, take a quite different view. He has argued that China's strategic importance has dramatically shrunk as a result of the dissolution of the Soviet Union. Not only are the ties that bind paltry in comparison to those that existed in the past, but China's cooperation in international matters concerning the Middle East, Cambodia or North Korea is neither essential nor reliable. Its aging leaders are out of tune with global developments and need to be confronted on the issues that divide us, not conciliated on the basis of illusions of past strategic importance.

One does not have to subscribe to either of these views to acknowledge that the strategic bottle is not as full as it once was. China's importance to the United States and vice versa has clearly been opened to question. The strategic relationship is simply no longer a "given": it can no longer either provide the crucial tie that binds, nor, more importantly, can it serve to obscure the deep differences that divide the two countries in other areas. It has become enmeshed in these other areas of growing contention.

Human Rights

The best example of how the post-Tiananmen environment has complicated a long-standing Sino-American problem is the question of human rights. Before the spring of 1989, it would have been difficult to imagine the prominent—almost preeminent—significance that the issue now holds. There were, of course, human-rights issues that divided the two countries. Allegations that China used forced abortion as a method of birth control led to confrontations at the UN as well as media charges and countercharges. The activities of the Dalai Lama in the United States and the intermittent congressional condemnation of Chinese policy in Tibet were important irritants in the relationship. Finally, in a manner reminiscent of the Soviet Union during the Leonid I. Brezhnev era (1964–82), there were signs that a nascent Chinese dissident movement might become a factor. In February 1989, an attempt by the American embassy in Beijing to invite the dissident Fang Lizhi to a reception in honor of President Bush was thwarted by Chinese public security officials, causing something of a stir in Sino-American relations.

However, it was only a stir. Neither side, particularly the Bush Administration, was prepared to allow human rights to become the issue it had once been in Soviet-American relations. In doing so, President Bush was continuing what UN Ambassador Jeane J. Kirkpatrick has called the "China exemption" in American human-rights policy, whereby each President since Nixon has striven to keep the issue in the background.

The shockingly visible Tiananmen brutality changed all this. The U.S. Congress took the lead in pressing the human-rights question and tying it to other issues in Sino-American relations. Each year since 1989, Congress has pressed the issue of Tibet and passed legislation linking MFN status with improvements in China's human-rights record. In addition, it has responded to the plight of the more than 30,000 Chinese students in the United States by seeking to legislate their status. Most recently, in May 1992, the Senate Judiciary Committee approved legislation that would allow those formerly on student visas to apply for permanent residency in 1993. Finally, during the summer of 1992, Congress appointed a commission to study the feasibility of establishing a "Radio Free Asia" intended to beam news into China, presumably at potential dissidents.

President Bush, on the other hand, has seemed torn between a desire to continue the policies of past Presidents and an awareness that the realities of the post-Tiananmen relationship render the former China exemption impossible. In reconciling these two priorities, the President's preference has clearly been for quiet diplomacy on the human-rights issue. For example, Secretary of State James A. Baker 3d, during his November 1991 visit, asked for the release of some of the 800 prisoners reportedly held by the Chinese. However, political realities have frequently forced President Bush to take more public stands, such as his spring 1991 meeting with the Dalai Lama or his direct rebuke to Premier Li Peng at their January 1992 meeting at the UN where he stated that "the record of the Chinese government on human rights was insufficient." These techniques, it was hoped, would acknowledge the pressures of Congress and public opinion while also signaling to the Chinese the importance of some accommodation on this issue in order to improve the relationship.

The Chinese leaders, however, have seemed unwilling to reach such an agreement. They have combined defiance with some willingness to engage in dialogue. Thus, even as Chinese leaders listen to foreign visitors, ranging from prime ministers to human-rights envoys, they play a curious cat-and-mouse game in response to American initiatives, whereby some dissidents are released and/or allowed to leave the country while still others are put on trial. Against the background of these few gestures of alternating concession and recalcitrance, the Chinese media have kept up a constant drumbeat of sharply worded statements—as well as a "white paper"—meant to disarm Western critics by "exposing" their record at home or by comparing the present domestic situation (particularly in Tibet) with that of the past. In regard to the former argument, the outbreak of violence in Los Angeles following the acquittal of the policemen implicated in the March 1991 beating of Rodney King and American policy toward Haitian refugees have, not unexpectedly, provided the material for extensive Chinese discussions. The Chinese have argued that except in very limited cases, human rights are a matter to be left up to individual nations to solve according to their own standards. For other states or an international body to interfere is not only a violation of national sovereignty, but a weapon in the arsenal of those who would undermine communism. China's leaders feel they have little flexibility in dealing with this issue, for to make concessions would only embolden the foreign and, perhaps of greater importance, the domestic enemies of communism.

The nature of global developments and of political pressures in both Washington and Beijing makes it unlikely that the human-rights issue will soon return to its secondary position in the relationship. The demands of public opinion, émigré Chinese groups and congressional critics require that it be placed in a prominent position by American policymakers and negotiators. For the Chinese, defiance is the predominant response to such actions; to do otherwise would constitute a sign of weakness at a time of increasing domestic and international pressures. Such defiance only heightens demands in the West that sanctions for unsatisfactory human-rights policies be imposed and promotes the linkage of this issue to others in relations with China. All of which, of course, only increases Chinese defiance—thus creating a vicious cycle.

Trade and Investment

In 1979, the year that diplomatic relations were established with the PRC, total Sino-American trade came to $2.3 billion and the structure for foreign investment was put in place by Chinese reformers. By the spring of 1989, two-way trade was close to $18 billion and American investors in China had pledged slightly over $3 billion for about 400 projects. The leading investors were from the colonies of British Hong Kong and Portuguese Macao; the U.S. share of investments was the largest among the world's nations.

With expectations of gain from the economic relationship running high on both sides of the Pacific, frustrations were inevitable. The Chinese looked to the United States as a source of essential technology, investment funds and export markets. By the late 1980s it seemed that Deng and his colleagues sought to replace the strategic dimension with the economic one as the core of Sino-American relations. However, what was perceived by Beijing as a cumbersome, as well as sometimes discriminatory, American licensing system seemed to prevent China from receiving more-advanced technology and to slow the shipment of approved items. Moreover, the rapid increase of textile exports to the United States had alarmed American producers and further aggravated growing protectionist sentiment, already inflamed by charges of Chinese dumping, that led to quotas being placed on Chinese textile exports.

These limitations were part of a broader issue that was particularly galling to the Americans. As Nai-Ruenn Chen of the U.S. Department of Commerce has noted, during the 1980s the growth in Sino-American trade was driven largely by burgeoning Chinese exports. Between 1983 and 1989 the U.S. trade deficit with China grew almost a hundredfold, from $71 million to $6 billion! It had become the sixth largest deficit on Washington's global trade account, and many American business people felt that Chinese conditions made it unlikely that this gap would be narrowed anytime in the near future. Imports were restricted, foreign currency was short in China and American businesses were frequently mired in bureaucratic red tape. Finally, the existence of a poorly articulated legal system, lacking protection of intellectual property such as computer software and riddled with "internal" rules invisible to foreigners, only increased frustrations.

The austerity campaign which began in the fall of 1988 served to aggravate the situation. The administrative clampdown restricted imports, limited the availability of foreign currency to Chinese buyers, curtailed credit to foreign corporations and disrupted American marketing and supply networks. Yet, despite all this, before the demonstrations at Tiananmen Square, the tone of Sino-American economic relations was, for the most part, upbeat. Most important, the overall healthy state of the relationship between the two countries seemed to ensure that many of these problems could be solved through bilateral negotiation in a manner isolated from politics. Each year, for nearly a decade, the President had, in the case of China, waived the provisions of the Jackson-Vanik amendment to the Trade Act of 1974 that requires nonmarket systems to permit freedom of emigration before being granted MFN status. This very political weapon, which remained leveled at the Soviets, was not allowed to intrude in Sino-American relations—until, that is, the events of June 1989.

Problems Continue to Plague Trade

Since that time there has been very little change in the *nature* of the economic issues that complicated bilateral relations. For example, the trade relationship has continued to be driven by Chinese exports to the United States. In 1990, China's exports to the United States increased by 27 percent, its imports of American goods dropped by 17 percent and the trade deficit reached $10.4 billion. In 1991, it was $12.7 billion, reaching the point where it was second only to Japan. (Some expect it to reach $15 billion to $20 billion in 1992.) Moreover, there were continuing complaints that Chinese tariffs and regulations (many of which were unpublished) made it unlikely that the balance could be redressed. It was further alleged that American corporations were losing close to $1 billion each year due to the Chinese failure to protect patents or copyrights on items ranging from pharmaceuticals to computer software to music recordings. Finally, there was evidence of the export of prison-made goods to the United States and of textiles falsely labeled as to brand or country of origin.

What *has changed*, of course, is the general context of the relationship that has served to politicize these economic differences and entwine them with other controversies through the MFN status granted to China in 1979 as a part of the process of normalization and a crucial factor in the export boom that followed. It was renewed on a yearly basis (before July 3) by executive order with hardly a stir in Washington. However, during the period 1990 to 1992, this all changed. The granting of MFN status became an area of contention between the Congress and the President. It also became the issue around which many of the differences over human rights, missile sales and trade practices seemed to coalesce.

For example, both the House (409–21, 11/26/91) and the Senate (59–39, 2/25/92) passed legislation requiring President Bush to certify that China was moving to release Tiananmen demonstrators, end proliferation of missile technology, stop the use of prison labor and lower barriers to imports as a precondition for the granting of MFN status. In the minds of many supporters of these bills, the Bush Administration's diplomacy had simply failed to affect any change in China's policies. As one columnist put it, unless an issue as vital as Chinese exports was used as "a pressure point for freedom," the leadership in Beijing would "keep thumbing their noses at the United States."

Those who opposed withholding MFN status doubted that such pressure would work and argued that it might actually run counter to certain other American interests. Many noted that if Chinese imports were limited, this would increase the cost of items ranging from clothing to electrical goods to shoes for American consumers. Moreover, Chinese retaliation by further limiting American imports would result in lost export sales of grain, aircraft and fertilizer. Restricting exports of Chinese origin to the United States would hurt precisely those forces that were continuing the drive toward a market economy in China—the joint ventures and small cooperative firms in the south—as well as innocent victims in the entrepôt of Hong Kong. By undermining these forces, the United States would actually be doing the work of those who sought to slow reform in China.

It was with this kind of reasoning that President Bush justified his successful veto of the 1991–92 congressional action. However, this did not settle the matter. In June 1992, Senator George J. Mitchell (D-Maine) introduced yet another bill setting the conditions for the granting of MFN in 1993. This bill, which passed the Senate and House in September 1992, is similar to the previous year's legislation except that it states that MFN would only be revoked for state-owned enterprises in China. Privately owned businesses or foreign joint ventures would be exempt from sanctions. Such targeted sanctions, it was argued, would not damage the interests of forces for reform in China. President Bush vetoed this bill, as well.

U.S. Hardens Policy

Although it has resisted these efforts, the White House has not been insensitive to the unpopularity of its policy toward China or to the potential political strength of the broad range of business and human-rights constituencies that have been pressing for a tougher stance. And when in June 1992 the President announced a renewal of MFN status, he also noted "insufficient" progress on human-rights issues. Indeed, over the previous year, Administration policy toward China had clearly hardened. Trade negotiators threatened to use provisions of the Section 301 of the Trade Act to increase tariffs on Chinese goods valued at over $1 billion if China did not make progress on the protection of copyrights and patents. In May 1992, federal prosecutors secured criminal indictments against Chinese trade officials who were accused of conspiring to avoid customs duties and taxes. As one official put it, "We're treating China like India or Indonesia or anyone else. In the old days, China was treated by different rules. Those days are gone."

With the United States taking almost one quarter of Chinese exports, Beijing had to respond to these problems in Sino-American trade. In certain areas it made concessions, promising greater protection of intellectual property, agreeing to curtail the export of prison-made goods, lowering of import barriers, improving means of identifying manufacturers of textile products, and sending buying missions to the United States. Indeed, by the summer of 1992 there were suggestions that concerns over the protectionist sentiments that would accompany a Democratic victory were prompting China's leaders to be more forthcoming on trade questions in talks with the Bush Administration. Still, their attitude on trade issues has also been defiant. China, as Foreign Minister Qian Qichen reaffirmed in addressing the Foreign Policy Association in New York City in September 1992, would never change policy in response to trade sanctions. On the crucial issue of MFN status, Chinese statements have consistently maintained that the granting of preferential tariff status was part of the basis for normalization of relations and should be kept separate from politics. Chinese leaders have responded to American pressure by threatening tariff retaliation and appear, on occasion, to have timed the trials of dissidents in a manner intended to demonstrate their indifference to American views. For example, even as the Senate voted in early 1992 on MFN status for China, sentences were announced for Chinese dissidents—one of whom was alleged to have been involved in the demonstrations at Tiananmen Square.

Finally, in Beijing, as in Washington, the trade issue has become linked to broader issues and has become politicized. An inner Communist party document leaked to Western reporters in late 1991 argued that the differences between President Bush and Congress were simply over means. Their ends were the same: "to make us collapse and bring about the peaceful evolution of socialist China." Although noting that the nation needed ties with other economies, the authors of this document asserted that American politicians who supported MFN status for China only did so because they saw it "as the most effective way to influence China's actions."

Chinese Foreign Minister Qian Qichen briefed a Foreign Policy Association audience on Sino-American relations, September 22, 1992.

©Elsa Ruiz

The Question of Taiwan

In 1949, the remnants of the defeated Nationalist regime which had retreated to Taiwan declared themselves to be the true government of China. After the outbreak of the Korean War, the United States gradually moved to a policy of military and diplomatic support for this claim. For the new Communist leaders of China, America's relations with Taiwan were seen as intervention in a domestic matter, plain and simple. In 1972, when Nixon went to China, mutual agreement on this issue was limited to the recognition that Chinese on both sides of the Taiwan Straits "maintain there is but one China and that Taiwan is a part of China." With the normalization of relations, Washington allowed its military alliance with the island to lapse and, although unofficial ties with Taiwan were maintained, diplomatic recognition shifted to Beijing.

Yet the matter continued to be a problem in the Sino-American relationship. The Chinese were suspicious that the

United States still sought to retain influence over Taiwan in order to frustrate reunification. A crisis was averted in 1982 with a joint communiqué in which Beijing stated that a peaceful settlement of the Taiwan issue was its "fundamental policy" and Washington pledged not to exceed in "qualitative or quantitative terms" the level supplied previously and to "reduce gradually" American arms sales to the island. In the years between this communiqué and the June 1989 demonstrations, the Taiwan issue remained an irritant in Sino-American relations, but it receded into the background. American policymakers had made it clear that so long as the issue remained peaceful, Taiwan's status vis-à-vis the mainland was a matter to be settled between the Chinese themselves. And this was precisely what seemed to be happening as relations between the formerly bitter enemies began finally to show some movement after more than three decades of confrontation.

Deng and his colleagues made the first gesture in 1979 when they stopped the periodic shelling of Nationalist-held islands. In the years that followed, the leaders in Beijing spelled out their program for Taiwan. Using the rough model of the British colony of Hong Kong, they pledged to accommodate the island under the principle of "one country, two systems." Taiwan would become a special administrative region of China with considerable control over domestic policies and an assurance that for 50 years its system could remain as it was. Although Beijing never absolutely renounced the use of force (and indeed sometimes sent quite threatening signals), it suggested that the military option would be reserved for quite specific cases, such as a move toward Taiwan independence, internal strife, the development of nuclear weapons, etc.

Officially, Taiwan remained unmoved by the mainland's overtures, standing by its announced policy of "three no's"— no contact, no talks and no compromises. However, beneath the veneer of this uncompromising stance, there were signs of some response from Taiwan symbolized by the growth of indirect Taiwanese trade and investment (largely through Hong Kong), as well as travel to the mainland. Indeed, representatives of the Taiwan media were in Beijing to record the events at Tiananmen Square via live broadcasts and eyewitness reports. Given the deep distrust that existed on both sides of the straits, the reactions to these events were predictable. In Taipei, the nation's capital, the army was put on alert, demonstrations were held at various universities, radio broadcasts to the mainland were increased, human-rights groups expressed outrage, and voices joined those throughout the world in condemning the actions of the Chinese army. In Beijing, there were charges of Taiwanese support for the demonstrators. However, there were also expressions of continued commitment to the development of trade with Taiwan and confidence that "more entrepreneurs from Taiwan will invest in China as they come to know the facts about the turmoil."

Taiwanese Trade and Tourism Soar

Indeed, this is precisely what happened. Western business people remained hesitant about investment and trade with China, and their colleagues from Taiwan rushed in. In the years since the Tiananmen crackdown, according to figures from Taiwan, two-way trade has grown by an average of about 40 percent a year, reaching more than $5 billion in 1991 (it is estimated to reach $7 billion in 1992), with a cumulative total reportedly in excess of $3 billion invested on the mainland. Exchanges in other areas have also grown. During 1991 there were more than 2.5 million Taiwanese visitors to the mainland (the figure rose to 3 million in 1992), and about 22,000 mainland residents visited Taiwan. Students from Taiwan were studying on the mainland, and athletes competed in the Asian Games held in Beijing in September–October 1990. On the other side of the straits, there was talk in Taipei of allowing mainland scientists to conduct research on the island and of recruiting scientists and technicians. Mail exchanges were reported to be averaging about 40,000 pieces a day, and one estimate in late 1991 put the number of cross-straits phone calls at 12 million during the previous two years. Finally, the institutional framework for regularized consultation was completed in December 1991 when Beijing established an "unofficial" body known as the Association for Relations Across the Taiwan Straits (ARATS) to deal with its Taiwanese counterpart, the Straits Exchange Foundation (SEF). Thirteen years after the shelling across the Taiwan Straits had stopped, the formerly bitter enemies were becoming connected by a growing web of economic and cultural relationships. Although the changed international environment had some part in explaining these dramatic developments, much of the impetus for change—as well as problems in the further development of the relationship—has come from within the two societies.

Although much attention has been given to China's reform decade, the 1980s also brought enormous economic and political changes to Taiwan. Its per capita gross domestic product (GDP) stood at more than 10 times that of China. With a population of 21 million, it had a GDP valued at more than one third that of the mainland (population 1.2 billion). The transformation of Taiwanese politics has been equally dramatic. Before his death in 1988, President Chiang Ching-kuo, the son of Chiang Kai-shek, had begun the process of political liberalization by lifting martial law and giving the opposition greater leeway. When power passed to his successor Lee Teng-hui, this process was accelerated. Lee, like three fourths of the island's citizens, was a native Taiwanese and his ascent to power had enormous symbolism for those of his compatriots who resented the mainland Kuomintang (Nationalist party, KMT)-dominated government which had arrived in the late 1940s. In 1991, he declared an end to the "Period of Communist Rebellion" that had justified the KMT's governance of the island under emergency rule. In the fall of the same year, open elections were held for a National Assembly whose function was to amend a constitutional system which had institutionalized one-party, mainland dominance of the island's policies. Running against the Democratic Progressive party which, in defiance of sedition laws, had called for the creation of a sovereign and independent Taiwanese state, the KMT won a landslide victory with 71 percent of the vote. As a government official noted, Taiwan had become "the first Chinese-dominated society to practice pluralistic politics."

Viewed from the mainland, the developments in Taiwan presented a mixed picture. In the economic realm, the desire of Taiwanese business people to expand some of their operations to the mainland was a positive development. Particularly at the height of post-Tiananmen sanctions, their willingness to fill many of the technological and investment holes left by the West was undoubtedly welcomed in Beijing. However, there were countervailing concerns: Taiwanese investment tended to be concentrated in labor intensive, low-tech industries; island people seemed to be promoting the "Taiwan experience" as well as business; and the concentration in the provinces of Fujian and Guangdong served to reinforce localism in these areas.

The Taiwan Challenge

The political evolution of the island, particularly the generational change that had occurred, presented a challenge to Deng and his colleagues. In the 1980s power had passed from the older, KMT leaders, who had maintained a deep spiritual attachment to the mainland, to a new generation of Taiwanese-born politicians to whom appeals for national unity had much less meaning and who seemed bent on staking out a distinctive place in the world. Pursuing what came to be called a flexible foreign policy, they enlarged the island's network of "unofficial" trade offices abroad (including even the nations of Eastern Europe and the former Soviet Union), expanded its foreign aid program and sought relations with countries that already recognized the mainland. Moreover, while the democratization of the island allowed Beijing to cultivate a constituency among business people, it also unleashed political forces for independence that were anathema to the leaders on the mainland.

To an aging mainland leadership, intent on settling a four-decades-long civil war, these were ominous developments. After 1989, Deng and his colleagues intensified their efforts to woo the government in Taiwan into negotiating the island's reunification with the mainland. However, at the same time there were continuing threats that Beijing reserved the right to use armed force in response to specific developments on Taiwan.

In the face of this campaign of the carrot and the stick, the government on Taiwan has played a cautious and skillful game. On the one hand, it has opened up unofficial channels of communication and has acceded to pressures from the business community as well as the mainland to permit expanded economic ties. Such an expansion not only made economic sense, but served to counter calls for Taiwan's independence. However, it has also kept the mainland at arm's length, claiming that the process of reunification should proceed in carefully delineated stages. Although there have been some recent discussions of a change in policy, Taipei's fears of the mainland gaining economic leverage have caused the government to continue to insist on *indirect* economic ties, with goods and deals going through third parties such as Hong Kong. It has also resisted mainland appeals for official government or party negotiation, maintaining that talks would have to await actions by Beijing such as the renunciation of force or the cessation of efforts to isolate Taiwan internationally.

For the KMT government this has proven a useful strategy. The growing economic and political gap between the mainland and Taiwan (made more visible by visits to the mainland) has considerably dulled popular enthusiasm on the island for immediate reunification, and there is not much enthusiasm for independence, either because of fear of mainland reaction or due to uneasiness with the idea of a Taiwanese nation. So for the moment President Lee and his

Under Taiwan's President Lee Teng-hui, tourism and trade with the mainland have been on the rise.

Reuters/Bettmann

colleagues seek the advantages of dialogue as they enjoy many of the benefits of *de facto* sovereignty. For Deng and his colleagues, this policy has created a deeply worrisome impasse. With the option of force constrained by military capabilities and the impact its use might have not only on world opinion but in triggering an American military response, they must play Taiwan's game. As they do so, the island's confidence and global influence grow—thus driving Beijing's dream of reunifying Taiwan with the mainland further into the future.

This apparent impasse has helped create a situation where the "Taiwan question" could once again become a divisive issue in Sino-American relations. In the United States, a few voices have been calling for a reconsideration of past policy. With Taiwan seeming to swim with the global tide of democratization and China resisting it, some wonder whether the old formulas are still appropriate. Most prominently, in the summer of 1991, former U.S. ambassador to China James Lilley questioned whether Chinese sovereignty over Taiwan might not have become "anachronistic," and argued that it was time to reexamine past policies. In the U.S. Congress, Senator Claiborne Pell (D-R.I.) sponsored the passage of a "revised bill on the destiny of Taiwan," insisting that any solution be "acceptable to the people of Taiwan." Even President Bush showed signs of a policy change. He pledged support for Taiwan's admission to GATT despite Chinese objections and, during the summer of 1992, he approved Taiwan's request, in response to growing concerns over Beijing's increased military capabilities, to purchase F-16 fighters. In doing so he reopened an issue that had been largely closed for a decade.

The Chinese reaction to American policy has been pointed and predictable. Not only were the fighter sales seen as an intervention in China's domestic politics, they were said to violate earlier Sino-American agreements on reducing arms sales to the island. Deng was reported to have approved "tough measures" in response, and one agricultural official suggested China might respond by halting American grain imports. Given their frustration with Taiwan's growing confidence, its dilatory responses to Beijing's initiatives and, most of all, the growing suspicion of American global policy, it was only natural that China's leaders would see American statements and actions as part of their problem in dealing with the island. For example, during the fall of 1991, there were suggestions in the Chinese press that Taiwanese aspirations for independence were being supported by forces in the United States that, like those practicing peaceful evolution, were seeking to return to past policies and "interfere in the affairs of the Chinese people." Although the electoral defeat of the proindependence party eased these concerns, the Taiwan question remains a delicate issue that is once again figuring prominently in Sino-American relations.

Dynamics of Sino-American Relations

No pictures could have had a greater impact on the American people than those of Chinese tanks toppling the Goddess of Democracy or of a lone citizen standing up to a column of tanks. For millions of viewers, it was the victory of totalitarianism over democracy and individual rights. Once more American illusions about China were shattered and Isaac's pendulum of American attitudes swung again—this time toward the "hate" pole. Moreover, as developments in Eastern Europe and the Soviet Union took their course, the image of "hard-line" China that originated at Tiananmen became even more strongly etched in the minds of the American people. The "hard-liners" in Beijing seemed to be bucking the trend of world democratization. In addition, many in the foreign policy community saw China's strategic importance significantly reduced with the demise of the U.S.S.R. as a global power. With the compelling issue of common opposition removed, the revulsion and distrust unleashed by Tiananmen seeped into all areas of the relationship.

In a similar fashion, the leadership's perception of the nature of Tiananmen within the context of the developing international environment profoundly shaped China's policy toward the United States. Almost immediately after Tiananmen, some of China's leaders fell back on their own stereotypes by linking the demonstrators with foreign forces seeking to undermine socialism. The nation was once again under siege from hostile, external forces.

Soon after the Tiananmen crackdown, President Bush took it upon himself to manage China policy, often with little regard to advisers inside or outside the executive branch. His policy was based on two elements: the personalization of policy and the imperative of maintaining a dialogue with China. The President argued that as a former envoy to China, he "knew" the country and its leaders sufficiently to manage the relationship. He has insisted that the greatest danger is that hostility toward China will force its leaders back to their isolationist posture of the past. Despite the political furor that arose as MFN status was renewed or envoys were dispatched, the President insisted that contact had to be maintained.

By making himself the creator of a very unpopular policy, President Bush has contributed to making China policy a partisan issue. Soon after the Tiananmen crisis, popular outrage was translated into a hardened congressional posture on China. In part, this was because changed conditions had made possible a widening of the traditional anti-China coalition to include human-rights and trade groups. However, it was also the result of party politics. The prominent role of Senate majority leader Mitchell in debates relating to China is evidence that, as one congressional staffer for a Democratic member put it, "China is a good issue for the Democratic party to make the President look bad." And such politics have not been without impact. The failed congressional override of the September 1992 veto of targeted MFN was due to the inability of the President's opponents to muster a two-thirds majority in the Senate (the vote was 59–40) after an overwhelming (345–74) victory in the House. If seven votes had changed in the Senate, Sino-American relations would have faced their most serious test of the past two decades.

One must be careful not to overestimate the extent to which congressional opinion and partisan politics have constrained American policy. Some of this has been political shadow play. For example, it was reported that the White House welcomed struggles with Congress that ended in a presidential veto simply because it aided the President's credibility with the Chinese. On the other hand, many Republicans and even some Democrats (particularly in the House) seemed willing to take the popular route of opposing China precisely because they knew that a presidential veto would stand. Some, it seems, were ready to vote with the President should that be needed.

Still, these elements of posturing should not obscure the fact that in the years since the Tiananmen Square crisis, Washington's China policy, for the first time since the Nixon trip of 1972, has become a partisan issue. For Democrats facing a President who campaigned for reelection on a record of foreign policy accomplishments, policy toward China was just too tempting a target. One exasperated policymaker summed up the situation when he said: "To a large extent, we're being driven by domestic considerations, which makes it hard to run a China policy." The enmeshing of America's China policy with domestic politics became evident as the presidential campaign began. Against a strong backdrop of protectionist sentiment, the Democratic party sharply criticized what they depicted as President Bush's failure to support forces promoting democratic reform. Democratic presidential aspirant Arkansas Governor Bill Clinton, in a major foreign policy address, chided the President for "signaling that we would do business as usual with those who murdered freedom in Tiananmen Square." Although the Administration continued to defend its China policy, there were hints of responsiveness to demands of election-year politics. Thus, during the Republican convention, it was announced that Chinese imports totaling $3.9 billion would be subject to "prohibitive tariffs" if there was no evidence by October that alleged trade barriers to American goods were being eased. Of greater possible consequence for Sino-American relations was the decision to sell F-16 fighters to Taiwan announced during a Bush campaign swing through Texas. This action, according to press reports, was prompted by charges from Democatic Senator Lloyd M. Bentsen Jr. of Texas that the refusal to sell planes to Taiwan was a cause of proposed layoffs at General Dynamics.

Concerns Over Western Ties

In China, domestic considerations are similarly influencing policy toward the United States. One such concern is leadership distrust of China's intellectuals and their vulnerability to foreign blandishments. It is no coincidence that soon after Tiananmen, Chinese statements seized upon Dean Acheson's comments that envisaged the emergence of "democratic individualists" who would turn China back toward the West. In 1949, although Mao ridiculed this statement, he took its message quite seriously. The concern about the domestic impact of closer ties with the West was a major factor conditioning his early insistence on attenuating ties. The spring 1989 demonstrations rekindled similar emotions in China's current leadership. Their fear of the impact of greater exposure to Western values has led them to pursue an often provocative policy toward the United States and to treat intellectuals as well as returning students with greater suspicion. This, in turn, has only further aggravated Sino-American relations.

Another domestic factor shapes China's policy toward the United States. There are serious shortcomings in the strength and outreach of the regime in Beijing that make it more difficult for its leaders to formulate and implement a cohesive national policy toward the United States. For example, the corruption or uncertain investment policies which often complicate Sino-American relations are frequently the result of an underdeveloped legal system. It is also probable that the national government finds it difficult to control the entrepreneurial economy in the south that is responsible for many of the trademark and labeling violations that have aggravated Sino-American relations. However, most serious in its consequences for Sino-American relations is the fact that international arms sales have become a lucrative source of income not simply for the Chinese military as an institution but for some offspring of influential Chinese. Some have argued that inconsistent or apparently duplicitous behavior ascribed to China's diplomats is a result of the foreign ministry's inability to control such important political forces.

Finally, as Harry Harding Jr. of The Brookings Institution has noted, there is also clear evidence that China's policy toward the United States is vulnerable to shifting divisions at the leadership apex. Although all Chinese leaders seem to harbor ambivalent attitudes toward the United States, some among the elite (for example, Chen Yun or Wang Zhen) have stressed the ominous side of their country's policy toward America in order to argue against the reformers and to promote their own policies and organizations. Their vision of a more-orthodox Communist domestic policy almost requires a weaker relationship with the United States.

There are other leaders who are more supportive of the opening to the West. Included here would be regional political figures in areas which have benefited enormously from foreign trade and investment (Shanghai and Guangdong, for example), and politicians who see a stable relationship with the United States as essential to the success of reform. Deng clearly falls in this latter camp. He is not any less concerned about the dangers of foreign subversion nor does he minimize the threat from the changing world order, but he is convinced of the need for China to get the wherewithal of development from abroad—particularly the United States.

In December 1991, as part of a broader campaign to diminish the influence of antireform elements and regain reform momentum, Deng is reported to have called for limiting the campaign against peaceful evolution, noting:

> We should not repeatedly mention the peaceful evolution plot by the West to change China's socialist system, because it goes against the United States. We need the United States to promote our reforms and openings. If we always confront the United States, we'll leave no leeway for us to maneuver.

In these ways, Chinese domestic politics influence the development of Sino-American relations. The direction of domestic policy in China is an important influence on how Beijing approaches the United States: a reform-minded leadership is more inclined toward the United States while less-reformist leadership leans toward confrontation. In the United States, policies and perceptions are strongly influenced not only by the approach but also by the general image projected by China. When China's reform seems to be moving smoothly, Washington is clearly more forthcoming than when it projects uncertainty and repression.

However, the lesson of the period since 1989 is that when events in China move in neither direction—or in both—the development of an American policy becomes more difficult. The fact that China's evolution is almost sure to defy the easy categorization with which many Americans feel most comfortable—Marxist adversary or capitalist friend—complicates the kind of understanding that is the basis for a sound American policy.

Conclusion

China is at a crossroads. In the near future, it will face
what has been a most difficult and complicated period
for any Leninist authoritarian regime—succession. Lacking
meaningful formal constitutional procedures, such systems
usually have passed through a period of intense political
manuevering—and often dramatic policy changes—before a
new leader or leadership team takes power. And more often
than not, the outcome of this process has defied the predictions of outside observers.

It also has defied the best intentions of the departed
leader, as the case of Mao Zedong made clear. In his last
years, Mao was deeply concerned about what would become
of the Chinese revolution after his death. In launching the
final revolutionary movement of his career—the Cultural
Revolution—he hoped to assure that subsequent leaders
would be worthy successors and that the imprint of his policies would be unalterably stamped on Chinese society.
Within three years of his death, Mao's designated successor
had been effectively neutralized as a political force and the

nation was embarked upon a course of reform that would dismantle much of his Communist vision.

This outcome certainly must humble anyone who would be so bold as to predict China's future. It also cannot bring much consolation to Deng Xiaoping as he confronts his passing. Like Mao in his last years, Deng is attempting to set a policy course that will endure beyond his death and will assure that those who succeed him stay the course. The vision of Chinese communism he would like to leave behind him is no less ambitious than that of Mao Zedong. He seeks to accomplish the reform of essential aspects of a Soviet-style economic system by means of a ruling Communist party. His effort will undoubtedly set the tone for Chinese politics not only during his last years but also for the succession period that follows.

China's Future: Reform and Succession

Any speculation on the course of China's most recent reform effort must proceed from a brief review of its motive force as well as its content. In regard to the question of motive force, this is very much Deng's effort—a fact which once again demonstrates the central role he has played in shaping the direction of post-Mao reform. Without holding a single public office, China's paramount leader by force of his own personality and prestige has been able to set the nation's political direction and to have it endorsed as the official party platform at the 14th party congress which met in October 1992. He has also exercised considerable influence in the process by which China's leaders are selected. Although he was apparently willing to tolerate Li Peng as premier and Jiang Zemin's leadership of the Communist party, Deng, in the past two years, has been supporting leaders sympathetic to his program. The most prominent among these, Zhu Rongji, the reformist vice premier, was promoted during the same congress to membership in the nation's most important ruling body, the seven-member Politburo Standing Committee.

Of course, Deng's efforts have also benefited from the specific circumstances of the fall of 1991. In the first place, demographics were in Deng's favor. Since the mid-1980s, China has been ruled by almost a shadow cabinet of Communist party elders who, while holding no or only honorific positions, have still made decisions at crucial junctures and supported clients in operational party-state positions. Many of these individuals have had strong reservations about continuing reform. However, they were also aging quickly, and several deaths among the Chinese elite during 1992 focused attention on reports that some of the more important conservative figures were becoming increasingly frail and infirm. Of course, there have also been rumors regarding Deng's health, and there can be little question that his very public trip to the south was intended to contrast his vigor with that of his colleagues.

However, it was not only the aging of his opponents that provided propitious conditions for Deng's efforts, but also the paucity of their program and the existence of constituencies favorably disposed toward new reform efforts. As several commentators have noted, by late 1991, more-conservative elements had little to show for their efforts. While they had been able to bring the economy under control, they were unable to mount a coherent alternative program that went much beyond political study and austerity. Almost by default, they had to allow much of the reform program to persist due to its success.

Almost, but not entirely. As Nicholas Lardy has argued, the reform program persisted also because it had the support of constituencies within China. Provinces, particularly those benefiting from foreign business, opposed any attempts to curtail reform. The rural population, as well as rural cadres, was clearly ill-disposed toward any curtailment of local industry or family farming. In the cities, a growing entrepreneurial middle class added its influence to more-general pressures to end the austerity measures and find a way to resume the pattern of rising living standards. Finally, many intellectuals, disgruntled with the narrowed post-1989 boundaries, looked for a rebirth of reform. Deng clearly tapped these constituencies when he launched his reform effort. In particular, he seemed to be banking heavily on support from those provinces that stood to gain from greater reform, or openness. Not only did he travel to the south to begin his effort, but he sought to solidify such support by increasing regional representation at the 14th party congress.

In short, the events of 1991–92 have shown that there still exist in China strong forces capable of resuming the march to reform. This would seem to substantiate the position of those Western observers who have contended that reform is irreversible in China—or, as some have said more graphically, now that the reform genie is out of the bottle, it cannot be returned. However, as events from Tiananmen Square to Warsaw to Moscow have demonstrated, to launch a reform movement is one thing; to have it stay the course or reach the objectives of its initiators is quite another.

Bureaucrats, seeking to protect prerogatives and sobered by past reversals, can be expected to respond slowly to the latest effort. Some of the interior provinces, with less to gain from foreign trade and investment, may not rally so quickly around the promise of increased decentralization. Although Deng's onslaught seems to have quieted his elite opposition, it persists. More importantly, it is prepared to exploit any difficulties that arise from reform efforts. And such difficulties are likely. Indeed, the *very factors* that have contributed to the launching of a reform effort contain within them elements that render its nature and outcome uncertain.

Not the least of these factors is the central role of Deng Xiaoping himself. Should Deng predecease certain of his colleagues—in particular the conservative Chen Yun—then his succession arrangement would certainly be jeopardized. Moreover, during the past decade Deng has shown that he himself is capable of upsetting succession arrangements when he finds his protégé wanting or he sees reform policies threatening his highly prized stability. Indeed, as his recent comments suggest, Deng's reform view continues to be dominated by his commitment to order, a factor that has caused him to curtail earlier efforts. In sum, Deng has proven to be a somewhat erratic reform leader.

China After Deng

The indispensability of Deng to the reform process raises obvious questions as to what will happen when he dies. Despite Deng's accomplishments at the 14th party congress, there was evidence of continued elite divisions. Moreover, it is impossible to predict how even his designated successors will behave when the cohesive force of his presence is gone and the succession struggle is in full swing. Very little is known about their views, and there is no assurance that in the heat of political struggle they will necessarily stand by positions taken during Deng's lifetime. The vague nature of Deng's program and the temptations of political expediency could move Deng's successors in unexpected directions, leading to a fragmentation of China's top leadership in the midst of the delicate process of reform.

With Deng not there to enforce elite conformity, other viewpoints and individuals will certainly emerge. For example, Deng's fellow elder, Yang Shangkun, has close ties to the military that have helped to make that institution supportive of reform efforts. How Yang and the military will behave in a succession period is uncertain. The same might be said of Qiao Shi, head of China's internal security apparatus, who has been similarly supportive of reform. Finally, the prominence of many sons and daughters of leaders has led some to speak of a future role for such "princelings." Although they did not fare well in the delegate elections to the 14th party congress, the personalistic quality of Chinese politics cautions against discounting their influence. One of the more interesting policy approaches that has grown out of such a group is associated with Chen Yun's son, Chen Yuan. Dubbed neo-conservatives by the Hong Kong press, they seek to combine authoritarian, more centralized rule with a reformed economy. There are sure to be other groups and platforms.

Deng will also leave another ambiguous legacy, a partially reformed political system that seems incapable of managing the kind of reform that is being proposed. The years since the Tiananmen crisis have demonstrated that the central government has the coercive power—the military, armed police, etc.—to maintain order and probably to avoid a collapse on the scale of Eastern Europe and the Soviet Union. China's present central political system can certainly maintain order. But can it do more?

The central government is not only overstaffed, poorly disciplined and short of funds, but it also sorely lacks the more subtle tools of governance needed if markets are to be introduced on a large scale and indirect state controls are to replace the Communist plan. Specifically, continued urban and rural reform will require a functioning civil service, an efficient national legal system, a national banking structure and an effective tax structure. Finally, the enthusiasm of middle levels of the bureaucracy for reform remains uncertain.

The bureaucracy is thus a blunt instrument. Once reform is under way, such a central government will have difficulties managing precisely the constituencies that have contributed to its initiation. The simple reason is that while these constituencies favor reform, it is reform on *their* terms. And these terms clash with the priorities of the national leadership. The outward-looking provinces of the south coast and perhaps those along the former Soviet border will surely use a period of reform to secure greater autonomy, develop their economies and gain a larger share of the national revenue pie. The growing entrepreneurial middle class will become less tolerant of inept or dishonest administration. While China's workers and urban residents welcome reform in the abstract, they have been unwilling to tolerate the corruption, inflation, lowered subsidies and, most of all, lessened job security that accompany it. They want the benefits of reform, but resist paying the price. With the Communist party's legitimacy based less on ideology and more on improved living standards, there will be even less tolerance of slower gains. Finally, past history suggests that intellectuals, chafing under the narrow definition of political reform, seek to push the leadership in directions, including greater political openness, that it does not wish to go. Even as they address existing problems, reforms create new tensions.

This was, of course, the lesson of 1988–89. But similar tendencies have emerged quickly in the initial period of the most recent reform effort. By the summer of 1992, the economies of the southern coast were booming once more. The rate of inflation was rising and the reported GNP growth rate of 12 percent suggested that the national economy might once again be overheating. There were also reports of a slowdown in the effort to introduce economic mechanisms into the state sector due to worker demonstrations and even attacks on managers by laid-off employees. Stock-exchange riots in Shenzhen suggested a tension between government corruption or caution and strong entrepreneurial instincts. Meanwhile, in the countryside there are reports of slowed growth in the standard of living and a widening, once more, of the gap between the city and the countryside. Finally, reports of unauthorized meetings of intellectuals to discuss freedom of the press or the struggle against "leftism" suggested that some intellectuals may, once again, be testing the reform waters.

Future Trends. Expectations are that the rhetoric of economic reform—learning from capitalism, introducing the market system, opening to the outside world—will dominate in the wake of the 14th party congress. The more-conservative themes of "peaceful evolution" and ideological study will be secondary. China will probably dramatically expand its economic ties to the outside world. Yet given the weaknesses in the Chinese polity and the conflicting expectations of reform, there will also be increasing tensions along three major faultlines: within the leadership; between the center and the provinces (perhaps between richer and poorer provinces, as well); and between the citizenry and their government.

The More Things Change...

How will these tensions be resolved? On the one hand, it seems unlikely that China will experience the same kind of generalized breakdown as occurred in Eastern Europe and the Soviet Union. Regionalism in China does not approximate the bitter ethnic separatism elsewhere, societal opposition remains weak, and, most important of all, the coercive powers of the party-state are likely to remain intact. On the other hand, it is equally unlikely that these difficult issues will be resolved smoothly and that reform will run its course. There are too many yet unsettled (or even undefined) questions—the limits of Communist party rule; the balance of power between central authorities and the localities; how elite politics will be structured after Deng's passing; etc. With so many unresolved—or even undefined—issues and no signposts to guide their resolution, China's reform future is likely to look very much like the past. A cautious, perhaps disunited leadership, armed with very blunt political instruments, will be attempting to carry out partial reform while confronting significant political pressures.

Under these circumstances, it is most likely that in the near term the political landscape will retain much of the complexity and many of the crosscurrents that have characterized it since the late 1980s. The center will be struggling with localities; the elite will be struggling with one another; market structures will be coexisting uneasily with the state-dominated economy as workers and entrepreneurs face rising prices and uncertain markets; students and intellectuals will be pressuring leaders committed to authoritarianism; growing foreign influence will still be viewed with suspicion by some. In this situation, policy will not only zigzag (perhaps punctuated by popular demonstrations met with repression), but it will also have the checkerboard-like quality that it has had over the past decade, with areas of reform existing alongside older patterns.

This is where the lessons of the post-Tiananmen period become relevant. Understanding China since the late 1980s has been much like the parable of the blind men and the elephant—depending on what part is touched, a very different animal is perceived. In the past, observers have seized upon different elements of the Chinese polity and economy at different points in time in order to make broad generalizations. Yet, as the instant wisdom after the Tiananmen demonstrations (as well as most of the prognostication since) has suggested, the zigzag and checkerboard quality of the Chinese reform has defied easy generalization—or labeling. A new attitude is necessary.

As the world has watched the tumultuous events in post-Communist Eastern Europe and the Soviet Union, it has become accustomed to systems of a highly ambiguous nature that defy easy categorization, as ethnic civil wars exist alongside uncertain democratization and stumbling economies. Earlier confidence that policies could be prescribed—or the future foretold—has diminished considerably. Although events in China in the near future will probably lack much of the drama and violence of those in other nations, they will have the same quality of change and ambiguity that defies easy stereotyping. If observers of China can eschew stereotypes and be open-minded to developments there, it would constitute a major reorientation in American attitudes that in the past have been dominated by wishful thinking and the desire to reshape China to suit American preferences.

Sino-American Relations and the New World Order

Sino-American relations, like China's domestic political order, are at a crossroads. There is a need to reassess the fundamentals of a relationship that has been shaken by both the global events accompanying the demise of the Communist states of Eastern Europe and the Soviet Union as well as the intense mutual hostility that suddenly erupted after the brutal and ugly events of June 1989. However, even as such fundamental questions are addressed, developments during 1992 (such as the arms sales to Taiwan, intensifying trade conflicts, and the pressures to create a "Radio Free Asia") are seriously complicating matters by adding the weight of immediate and sharply divisive issues to an already shaky foundation of bilateral relations.

On the Chinese side, there seems ample motivation to resolve these immediate tensions and to seek the bases of a new Sino-American relationship. The mainstream of Chinese leadership, led by Deng Xiaoping, remains committed to the policy of an economic open door and sees the United States as playing a crucial role in its success. There is also a continued appreciation of the importance of good relations with the United States in the maintenance of a benign strategic environment that will allow a focus on economic growth. Although Chinese commentaries cite the multipolar nature of the post-cold-war world, there seems to be an appreciation of the present American strategic preeminence. This is particularly the case in the Asian region. American influence is seen as crucial not only to the settlement of the Taiwan question and the resolution of tensions between north and south on the Korean peninsula, but also as a counterweight to growing Japanese economic and perhaps even military influence in the region.

Yet, even as China's leaders promote such a reassessment, the new global context and the course of domestic politics complicate its achievement. For example, while the international orientation of the reform effort would surely incline Deng and his colleagues to seek an easing of tensions, the unfolding of the reform process itself might ironically result in a greater perception of foreign intervention on the part of the Chinese leadership. Expanded export growth will bring greater scrutiny of China's domestic economy and legal system. Attempts by coastal areas to develop ties with the outside world (as well as Taiwan) and to exploit these ties for greater autonomy from Beijing could easily be perceived as attempts by outside forces to detach parts of China. Finally, the persistence of a very restrictive definition of political reform, and the likelihood that Deng will deal harshly with any signs of instability, will certainly invite "interference" on human-rights issues.

China's appreciation of the global influence of the United States is tempered by an uneasiness that is felt even by those Chinese leaders most committed to an open-door policy. The events at Tiananmen and the American reaction that followed revealed China's vulnerability to external currents and the readiness of politicians in the United States to use economic and cultural policies to affect change in China. The rhetoric of the new world order, Washington's open support of the "democratic revolution" in formerly Communist states, and pressures on human-rights issues have only increased concerns on this score.

This uneasiness on the part of Deng and his supporters defines the boundaries within which they have been willing to explore both a resolution to immediate tensions as well as the new bases for a Sino-American relationship. With the United States playing such an important role as an importer of the nation's manufactured goods and a supplier of technology, the limits and costs involved in confronting Washington have been clear. This was undoubtedly a factor promoting an October 1992 agreement to reduce Chinese trade barriers that avoided the American sanctions threatened earlier in the summer. Moreover, the exigencies of reform (as well as concern over a Democratic victory in the presidential election) may have moderated Chinese responses to the human-rights issues and arms sales to Taiwan.

However, such moderation has its limits. Over time, weighing perceived affronts to China's national rights against the economic worth of the Sino-American relationship may well take its toll. Deng's deep commitment to China's sovereign rights, intensified by frustration over perceived American use of economic leverage as well as pressures from more-conservative elements in the Communist party, will condition more prickly responses to issues that are perceived as holding China to a different standard or—as in the case of arms sales to Taiwan or human rights—as interfering in its domestic politics. For example, Beijing's decision not to attend UN talks on arms control in the Middle East can be seen as one such response.

U.S. Reassessment

From the American point of view, there is also reason to settle existing tensions and move to the more fundamental work of exploring the bases for a new post-cold-war relationship with China. It is a permanent member of the UN, with veto power. China's status as a major arms dealer and nuclear power means that its policies should command similar attention in regard to questions of nuclear proliferation and regulation of weapons sales. Its sheer size, as well as its specific policies in regard to questions ranging from birth control to the use of bituminous coal, is relevant to recent efforts toward global cooperation on the environment, population and disease control. At a time when American policy in the Asian Pacific region is undergoing a fundamental reconceptualization, the uncertain evolution of China's politics is not only part of the problem—it is also part of the solution. Finally, of course, bilateral factors ranging from the considerable American economic stake in China to the less finite American preoccupation with China are all factors that would seem to stimulate a reassessment.

Yet, the formulation of policy in Washington—as in Beijing—has been complicated by international as well as domestic factors. In recent years, the configuration of international forces and alliances in Asia has undergone some of its most dramatic realignments since World War II. The Soviet Union is no more. However, the Central Asian successor-states have remained an important factor due to their strategic location and natural resources. Russia remains deeply involved in Asia on a broad front ranging from contacts with Taiwan to the yet-unsettled dispute with Japan over islands seized in 1945 to the massive Asian presence symbolized by Siberia. Finally, two economic giants—Japan and South Korea—have begun to play a more active political role in the region.

Indeed, the very definition of "China" has been changing since Tiananmen even as Asia has changed. As commentators such as Gerald Siegal of the International Institute of Strategic Studies have noted, different regions of China seem to be oriented to different parts of Asia : the northern interior regions look to Russia, the northern coastal provinces to South Korea and Japan, etc. However, among these, the most important seems to be the linkage that has become known as Greater China—the network of ties that have developed between the provinces of Fujian and Guangdong, the British colony of Hong Kong (due to revert to China in 1997) and Taiwan. Although the economic weight of these ties suggests that they should figure importantly in the making of American policy, it has not been an easy matter to integrate them into overall policy. Congressional action, supported by the Administration, intended to treat Hong Kong "as a separate territory" even after it reverts to China in 1997, has been angrily rejected by Beijing. Moreover, with business people from Hong Kong and Taiwan investing in China's southern provinces and reexporting goods made there, the implications of economic sanctions have become more complicated. Such sanctions would not only hurt more-entrepreneurial elements in China—they would damage the interests of those outside the country.

In this complex international environment, the domestic politics of the United States has influenced foreign policy. President Bush has advocated the need to avoid isolating China, and the Democratic party, responding to pressures from trade, human-rights and Chinese émigré organizations, as well as the temptations of partisan politics, pressed for a more punitive policy. The exigencies of election-year politics limited the Bush Administration's room to maneuver on

human-rights and trade issues and moved it to take clearly provocative actions such as the arms sales to Taiwan.

However, it seems unlikely that either the politicized quality of the China question or the fundamental post-1989 American perceptions of the world and China will change significantly soon. If the experience since Tiananmen is any guide, the American response to the unfolding of Deng's last reform effort will assure that ambivalence continues to shape the relationship on this side. On the one hand, reform may, once again, raise American expectations that China is joining the global trend toward "liberalization" or "capitalism." On the other hand, the reality of the country during the end of Deng's rule will most likely be very much as it has been during the post-1989 period—a complex amalgam of genuine reform and reaction, with the potential for upheaval and repression.

Looking farther ahead, after Deng's death the issue of policy toward the United States is likely to be embedded in broader differences over the future of the reform movement. The new leadership will undoubtedly come under increased political pressure from both conservatives who would like to restrict ties with the outside world as well as regional forces seeking broadened ties. Although the initial instincts of Deng's successors are likely to be inclined toward a continuation of Deng's economic policies and thus a more accommodating posture toward the United States as major economic support of China's reform effort, there are numerous factors that might move policy in a much different direction.

Transition: A Time of Uncertainty

In the past, periods of political uncertainty have usually engendered fears of outside intervention on the part of China's leaders. Should disturbances break out or provinces use the occasion of leadership transition to enlarge their privileges, then one might expect aspiring leaders to react sharply to such perceived or real attempts at interference. Finally, succession brings political posturing and opportunism. Aspiring leaders could mobilize support behind appeals to nationalism that could touch upon a wide range of issues, from Taiwan to the disputed islands in the Pacific and South China Sea to cultural and economic penetration.

Should attitudes remain what they have been in the past, such an evolution of Chinese politics will leave very little room for a fundamental reassessment from the American side. Those seeking to maintain contacts with China will still have elements of continued economic reform and some flexibility on economic and security issues to strengthen their case. However, it also seems likely that a defiant, unsettled and still repressive atmosphere will provide much grist for those who argue for more distance in the relationship and greater pressure on the Chinese for change.

Indeed, during a post-Deng succession the bases for such a position might actually increase, not simply because the chances for repression will increase, but because the chances for affecting political change in China also will appear to have increased. Not only will there be temptations to direct American policy toward the support of more "progressive" leaders, but there might be talk of giving special encouragement or support to some of the exporting provinces in the southern part of China that seem particularly oriented toward the United States. If past history is a guide, such attempts to change China from the outside will not only fail, but in a postsuccession atmosphere of vulnerability and nationalism, they could be used to drum up patriotic opposition to outside interference and throw relations into yet another crisis.

The near future yields little promise of regaining the apparent serenity of past Sino-American relations. The special quality that has characterized the relationship and cushioned or obscured so many potential conflicts is gone. The areas where bilateral differences must be resolved—trade, human rights, Taiwan, etc.—are significant ones. It is not so much that the issues which divide the two nations are necessarily insoluble; rather it is that there is little promise that the assumptions and domestic political environments on both sides of the Pacific will be such as to promote their resolution in the relatively smooth fashion that often characterized the period before Tiananmen.

Yet this is not necessarily a pessimistic conclusion. A future in which the United States and China view each other as they are and not as they wish each other to be would be a significant change from the past. While a relationship without illusions, built out of conflict, would lack the equilibrium or even the stability of the past, it might be less volatile. As Steven I. Levine, a prominent observer of Chinese foreign policy, has argued, despite the severe traumas of the post-Tiananmen period, Sino-American relations have demonstrated the resilience that might make such a transition possible. A network of economic, cultural and political ties has persisted. And more importantly, there is ample evidence that there exists on both sides of the Pacific a minimum of common interest and will to promote relations that not only have acted to control the damage of the past three years, but which, along with the established network of ties, could sus-

tain efforts to manage what portends to be a far more difficult relationship in the decade ahead.

Talking It Over

A Note for Students and Discussion Groups

This issue of the HEADLINE SERIES, like its predecessors, is published for every serious reader, specialized or not, who takes an interest in the subject. Many of our readers will be in classrooms, seminars or community discussion groups. Particularly with them in mind, we present below some discussion questions—suggested as a starting point only—and references for further reading.

Discussion Questions

Some have argued that when China's leaders confronted the demonstrators in Tiananmen Square during the spring of 1989, they were, in fact, confronting the consequences of their own reforms. What would be the bases for such a judgment?

Why has it proven so difficult to reform Soviet-style Communist systems such as that which developed in China after 1949?

In what areas did the reforms of 1978–89 bring about the greatest changes in the system that existed when Mao died? In what areas was there the least change? Why do you think change took the particular path that it did from 1978 to 1989? What factors account for the course that China took in the period after Tiananmen? Is there anything to be learned about the future of China from the years since the summer of 1989?

In what ways has the Chinese view of the world changed in the years since Mao's death? What aspects of the perceived changes have China's leaders considered advantageous for their nation? What have they considered to be disadvantageous? Do all Chinese leaders agree with these assessments?

What accounts for the worsening of Sino-American relations in the years since Tiananmen? What developments might contribute to an improvement in the relationship? What developments might make things worse?

What seems to be the most likely future—or futures—for the development of the Chinese system? What are the bases for this judgment? Are there ways in which outsiders can shape such a process?

READING LIST

Amnesty International, *China: The Massacre of June 1989 and Its Aftermath.* New York, Amnesty International, 1989. A report on the events at Tiananmen Square and the arrests that followed.

Barnett, A. Doak, *After Deng, What?* Washington, D.C., The Johns Hopkins Foreign Policy Institute, 1991. A brief introduction to the issues that will face China in the future.

Ch'i, Hsi-sheng, *Politics of Disillusionment: The Chinese Communist Party Under Deng Xiaoping, 1978–1989.* Armonk, N.Y., M.E. Sharp, Inc., 1991. A political history of Deng Xiaoping's reform effort in these years.

Current History, September 1992. Entire issue devoted to China,1992, as seen by eight experts.

Harding, Harry, *A Fragile Relationship: The United States and China since 1972.* Washington, D.C., The Brookings Institution, 1992. An assessment of the past two decades of Sino-American relations.

———, *China's Second Revolution: Reform After Mao.* Washington, D.C., The Brookings Institution, 1987. Although somewhat dated by now, this remains the best study of the first decade of post-Mao reform politics.

Joseph, William A., *China Briefing, 1991.* Boulder, Colo., Westview Press, 1992. A series of essays published yearly covering China's domestic and foreign policies.

Lardy, Nicholas, *Foreign Trade and Economic Reform in China, 1978–1990.* New York, Cambridge University Press, 1992. The development of foreign trade policy within the context of post-Mao economic reform.

Link, Perry, *Evening Chats in Beijing: Probing China's Predicament.* New York, Norton, 1992. An American academic listens to—and looks at—China's intellectuals.

MacFarquhar, Roderick, and Fairbank, John K., eds., *The Cambridge History of China*, Vol. XIV, *The People's Republic of China*, Part 1, *The Emergence of Revolutionary China, 1949–1965.* New York, Cambridge University Press, 1987. Leading specialists view political, social and economic developments in China in the period from the victory of the Communist party until the Cultural Revolution.

————, *The Cambridge History of China*, Vol. XV, *The People's Republic of China*, Part 2, *Revolutions Within the Chinese Revolution, 1966–1982.* New York, Cambridge University Press, 1991. China from the Cultural Revolution through the post-Mao succession.

Oi, Jean, *State and Peasant in Contemporary China: The Political Economy of Village Government.* Berkeley, University of California Press, 1989. A discussion of the nature of the rural political economy from the collectivization of the mid-1950s through the reforms of Deng Xiaoping.

Oksenberg, Michel, and Lambert, Marc, eds., *Beijing Spring, 1989: Confrontation and Conflict: The Basic Documents.* Armonk, N.Y., M.E. Sharpe, 1990. Contains commentary covering not only the events of 1989 but also some of their origins.

Saunders, Harold, *et al., Tibet: Issues for Americans.* New York, National Committee on United States-China Relations, April 1992. Report on conditions in Tibet, written by a study group headed by a former State Department official.

Shambaugh, David, *Beautiful Imperialist: China Perceives America, 1972–1990.* Princeton, N.J., Princeton University Press, 1991. How China's "America-watchers" see us.

Spence, Jonathan, *The Search for Modern China.* New York, Norton, 1990. A survey of Chinese history from the fall of the Ming dynasty in the seventeenth century to the 1989 events at Tiananmen.

U.S. Congress, Joint Economic Committee, *China's Economic Dilemmas in the 1990s; The Problems of Reforms, Modernization, and Interdependence,* Vols. 1 & 2. Washington, D.C., U.S. Government Printing Office, 1991. Leading academic and government specialists examine various aspects of China's domestic politics, economic policies and international economic relations.

Whiting, Allen S., special editor, *Annals of the American Academy of Political and Social Science,* Vol. 519, January 1992. A collection of essays by leading specialists on China's foreign relations.

Statement of Ownership, Management and Circulation

UNITED STATES POSTAL SERVICE

(Required by 39 U.S.C. 3685)

1A. Title of Publication	1B. PUBLICATION NO.	2. Date of Filing
Headline Series	0 0 1 7 8 7 8 0	9/30/92

3. Frequency of Issue	3A. No. of Issues Published Annually	3B. Annual Subscription Price
Quarterly: Winter, Spring, Summer, Fall	Four	$15.00

4. Complete Mailing Address of Known Office of Publication *(Street, City, County, State and ZIP+4 Code) (Not printers)*

Foreign Policy Association, 729 Seventh Avenue, New York, NY 10019

5. Complete Mailing Address of the Headquarters of General Business Offices of the Publisher *(Not printer)*

Same as above

6. Full Names and Complete Mailing Address of Publisher, Editor, and Managing Editor **(This item MUST NOT be blank)**

Publisher *(Name and Complete Mailing Address)*

Foreign Policy Association, 729 Seventh Avenue, New York, NY 10019

Editor *(Name and Complete Mailing Address)*

Nancy Hoepli, Same as above

Managing Editor *(Name and Complete Mailing Address)*

N/A

7. Owner *(If owned by a corporation, its name and address must be stated and also immediately thereunder the names and addresses of stockholders owning or holding 1 percent or more of total amount of stock. If not owned by a corporation, the names and addresses of the individual owners must be given. If owned by a partnership or other unincorporated firm, its name and address, as well as that of each individual must be given. If the publication is published by a nonprofit organization, its name and address must be stated.) (Item must be completed.)*

Full Name	Complete Mailing Address
Foreign Policy Association	729 Seventh Avenue, New York, NY 10019

8. Known Bondholders, Mortgagees, and Other Security Holders Owning or Holding 1 Percent or More of Total Amount of Bonds, Mortgages or Other Securities *(If there are none, so state)*

Full Name	Complete Mailing Address
N/A	N/A

9. For Completion by Nonprofit Organizations Authorized To Mail at Special Rates *(DMM Section 424.12 only)*
The purpose, function, and nonprofit status of this organization and the exempt status for Federal Income tax purposes *(Check one)*

(1) ☒ Has Not Changed During Preceding 12 Months	(2) ☐ Has Changed During Preceding 12 Months	*(If changed, publisher must submit explanation of change with this statement.)*

10. Extent and Nature of Circulation *(See instructions on reverse side)*	Average No. Copies Each Issue During Preceding 12 Months	Actual No. Copies of Single Issue Published Nearest to Filing Date
A. Total No. Copies *(Net Press Run)*	8,463	8,000
B. Paid and/or Requested Circulation 1. Sales through dealers and carriers, street vendors and counter sales	792	584
2. Mail Subscription *(Paid and/or requested)*	3,149	2,598
C. Total Paid and/or Requested Circulation *(Sum of 10B1 and 10B2)*	3,941	3,182
D. Free Distribution by Mail, Carrier or Other Means Samples, Complimentary, and Other Free Copies	500	500
E. Total Distribution *(Sum of C and D)*	4,441	3,682
F. Copies Not Distributed 1. Office use, left over, unaccounted, spoiled after printing	4,022	4,318
2. Return from News Agents		
G. TOTAL *(Sum of E, F1 and 2—should equal net press run shown in A)*	8,463	8,000

11. **I certify that the statements made by me above are correct and complete**

Signature and Title of Editor, Publisher, Business Manager, or Owner

[signature] Managing Director, Administration

PS Form **3526**, January 1991   *(See instructions on reverse)*